The Church's Response to Domestic Violence

Dr. Char M. Newbold

Carpenter's Son Publishing

Edited by Tiarra Tompkins and Ann Tatlock

Cover and Interior Design by Suzanne Lawing

Printed in the United States of America

ISBN: 978-1-952025-48-8

This study is written by a survivor,
one who has walked through the fire of domestic violence
and has come out not even smelling like smoke
because He was and is with me.

It is dedicated to all the women who
have been broken and all those God uses to help.

Note: For the purpose of this work, "survivor" and "victim" will be used interchangeably. Because my experience is almost exclusively with women who have men abusers and because this study is designed for women, the terms "survivor" and "victim" will reference women and "abuser" will reference men. I also have used the terms "domestic violence" and "intimate partner violence" interchangeably.

Although this book focuses on women because women are the majority who suffer in these situations, that is not to negate or downplay the abuse that men also experience with domestic violence. I have known women to be the aggressors and have seen men suffer the same experiences and damage as women who have been abused. The victim stories related within these pages are as I recall them and as they have been shared with me. Many of the victim stories could be interchangeable with males or females as victims.

Disclaimer: The sections of this book that contain advice and instruction are meant to be guidelines. There is no replacing proper tools and training for handling small groups or one-on-one domestic violence situations.

Many Thanks

To my Lord, Jesus Christ: I give my deepest thanks. Without You, I can do nothing.

To my family, church families, and friends: my journey from then to now would have been very different without your prayers, financial support, and love.

To my personal advocates: thanks for lending me your strength when I had none. You share in the victory of every woman who is set free from domestic violence through this work.

To the Purple Posse: you bless me with your incredible strength. You are all amazing!

To my daughter: you have been my biggest motivation to live a safer, healthier life. From your birth, you have offered joy, support, wisdom, and humor. You are my precious gift from God.

To my husband: there is no one who has encouraged me more than you to finish this writing. Your support has been incredible.

To God be the glory.

Table of Contents

Why Am I Writing This Book?

The face of domestic violence might surprise you. If you read my credentials—a respected teacher, a leader in a local church, a Sunday School teacher, a highly educated woman, an experienced public speaker, and an advocate for child abuse victims—you wouldn't suspect that I was a victim of domestic violence. If you had asked me back then if I was being abused, I would have answered with a resounding, "No!" Why? Because I did not believe I was. On my honest days, I would have said my husband had a drinking problem or anger issues. The common misconception about abuse is it means "he hits you." He never broke any bones or put me in the hospital, so he would have told you he wasn't abusive either. Truth be told, he treated me better than his dad treated his mom.

Having grown up in an upper middle-class neighborhood with two loving parents who raised me in church and never resorted to violent behavior in the home, I had no experience with abusive behavior. If you had asked me what an abusive relationship looked like, I would have given you the same cliché we've seen in the movies for decades: the bruised and battered woman unable or unwilling to leave her relationship. I was a married Christian with a good job, a beautiful child, and close friends. I couldn't be a victim of domestic violence …yet I was.

Only with the help of domestic violence advocates and a support group for victims did I begin to understand that my former husband exhibited the behavior of an abuser. Worse, I exhibited the behavior of a victim. The realization didn't come easily. Because he never raised his hand to hit me and I didn't have to explain away injuries, I was in denial about his abuse. With time, I came to realize I had been abused in more ways than one. The physical, emotional, financial, and even sexual abuse had gone on longer than I had known. The once subtle signs I had brushed off were now glaring warning signs. With recognition of abuse comes shame and blame. I gradually learned to switch my thinking from blaming myself and continually trying to fix our relationship to understanding that I was not responsible for his behavior. I also came to understand that I deserved a better life than the one I had with him. With the additional help of my supportive family and friends, I grew to believe in my value as a woman and as a child of God. Encouraged, I grew closer to Him and drew my strength from Him.

> *"It is God who arms me with strength,*
> *and makes my way perfect." Psalm 18:32 NKJV*

As with any major life event, everyone has an opinion about what is right and wrong. Along the way, misguided, uninformed religious leaders and fellow Christians gave me a variety of bad counsel. I am so grateful for the divine appointment leading me to the man of God who correctly counseled me spiritually while I was still in my relationship, every time I left, and after I left for good. He taught me to study the Word and develop the ability to hear God for myself. As I began to understand the truth of God's Word and His love for me, I gained the courage to leave and the grace to heal. Thanks, Pastor.

I now consider myself a survivor, not a victim. Yes, bad things happened to me, but I don't let them define who I am now. In the later stages of my own journey to wholeness, God spoke to me about helping others.

> *"Speak up for those who cannot speak for themselves; ensure justice*
> *for those being crushed. Yes, speak up for the poor and helpless, and*
> *see that they get justice." Proverbs 31:8-9 NLT*

This guide is part of my obedience to Him. My sincere prayer is that through these pages, the women who come to the faith community for help will experience the heart of God for those being crushed. And as His servants, let us minister to the spiritual, physical, and emotional needs of the victims of domestic violence seeking our help, from first disclosure to extended care.

Let the Church arise as beacon of hope.

"For I know the plans and thoughts that I have for you, says the LORD, plans for peace and well-being and not for disaster to give you a future and a hope." Jeremiah 29:11 AMP

Chapter 1

How Is the Church Responding to Domestic Violence?

*They offer only superficial help for the harm my people
[daughters] have suffered. They say, 'Everything will be all right!'
But everything is not all right! Jeremiah 6:14 NET*

When bad things happen, it is so easy to succumb to feelings of abandonment and unworthiness. No matter what the hurt, each of us has wondered the big question, "Why me?" A person of faith experiencing violence in the home is experiencing not only abuse, but a crisis of faith. As a believer, the effects of domestic violence create a crisis in her soul and the target is her faith. She questions her basic tenets of faith: Where is God? Why does God let this happen to me? Is God punishing me?

God's daughters are crying out in suffering. Where is the church?

We, the Christian faith community, have the opportunity to direct her to our source of strength and hope: the Word of God. Scriptures in no way justify abuse. The church must be the clear voice for taking a stance against domestic violence. This is not about the sanctity of marriage but the sanctity of life. We can no longer allow what goes on in the privacy of the home to remain private when abuse is occurring. Our women and children are dying at the very hands of those who are supposed to protect them. God's children were not called to live and die in silence to preserve marriage. These deadly marriages must be attributed truthfully to the violence done by the hands of abusers.

Isaiah 56:10-11 talks about the watchmen who are blind because they are without knowledge. They are shepherds that lack understanding.

> *His watchmen are blind; they are all without knowledge;*
> *they are all silent dogs; they cannot bark, dreaming, lying down,*
> *loving to slumber. The dogs have a mighty appetite;*
> *they never have enough. But they are shepherds who have no*
> *understanding; they have all turned to their own way, each to his*
> *own gain, one and all. Isaiah 56:10-11 ESV*

Many watchmen shepherds (church leaders) lack knowledge and understanding in the area of domestic violence. Domestic violence is real, and we cannot serve Christ and ignore those He called us to serve and protect.

- In the United States, an average of 20 people experience physical violence from an intimate partner every minute. This adds up to more than 10 million abuse victims annually.[1]

- 1 in 4 women and 1 in 9 men experience severe intimate partner physical violence, intimate partner contact sexual violence, and/ or intimate partner stalking with impacts such as injury, fearfulness, post-traumatic stress disorder, use of victim services, contraction of sexually transmitted diseases, etc.[2] This is commonly considered "domestic violence."

  - 1 in 3 women and 1 in 4 men have experienced some form of physical violence by an intimate partner. This includes a range of behaviors and in some cases might not be considered "domestic violence."[3]

- 1 in 7 women and 1 in 25 men have been injured by an intimate partner.[4]

- 1 in 10 women have been raped by an intimate partner. Data is unavailable on male victims.[5]

• 1 in 7 women and 1 in 18 men have been stalked. Stalking causes the target to fear she/he/they or someone close to her/him/them will be harmed or killed.[6]

• On a typical day, domestic violence hotlines nationwide receive over 20,000 calls.[7]

• An abuser's access to a firearm increases the risk of intimate partner femicide by 400%.[8]

• Intimate partner violence accounts for 21% of all violent crime.[9]

• Intimate partner violence is most common against women between the ages of 18-24.[10]

• 19% of intimate partner violence involves a weapon.[11]

• 1 in 3 female murder victims and 1 in 20 male murder victims are killed by intimate partners.[16]

• A study of intimate partner homicides found 20% of victims were family members or friends of the abused partner, neighbors, persons who intervened, law enforcement responders, or bystanders.[17]

• 72% of all murder-suicides are perpetrated by intimate partners.[18]

• 94% of murder-suicide victims are female.[19]

• Victims of intimate partner violence are at increased risk of contracting HIV or other STI's due to forced intercourse and/or prolonged exposure to stress. [20]

- Intimate partner victimization is correlated with a higher rate of depression and suicidal behavior.[21]

- Only 34% of people who are injured by intimate partners receive medical care for their injuries.[22]

- Victims of intimate partner violence lose a total of 8 million days of paid work each year, the equivalent of 32,000 full-time jobs.[23]

- Intimate partner violence is estimated to cost the US economy between $5.8 billion and $12.6 billion annually, up to 0.125% of the national gross domestic product.[24]

- Between 21-60% of victims of intimate partner violence lose their jobs due to reasons stemming from the abuse.[25]

- Between 2003 and 2008, 142 women were murdered in their workplace by former or current intimate partners. This amounts to 22% of workplace homicides among women.[26]

These statistics are staggering. Women and children who are abused can escape death at the hands of the abuser but are often wounded emotionally and physically for life. The danger is real. The pain and suffering are real. Statistically, it is a reality for approximately one-third of our female congregation.[27] Sadly, less than 30% of pastors believe abuse is a problem in their church.[28]

Are We Listening?

Who will listen to their story? Who will exhibit the comfort of a caring, compassionate Christ? Who will offer a safe haven? Who will stand beside them? Who will advocate for their lives? Who will insist on accountability for abusers while interceding for their souls?

We, the Church, are failing our families who are experiencing violence in the home. It is not an easy topic to discuss, but it is time to get out of our comfort zone and show the love of Christ. It's time to minister to the hurting and broken victims of domestic violence.

How the Church Can Help Victims and Their Families

We need to admit there is a problem. We can no longer turn a blind eye; lives and futures are at stake. A total of 87,000 women were intentionally killed in 2017. More than half of them (58%) 50,000 were killed by intimate partners or family members, meaning that 137 women across the world are killed by a member of their own family every day. More than one-third (30,000) of the women intentionally killed in 2017 were killed by their current or former intimate partner, someone they would normally expect to trust.[29] Let us advocate for the innocent: the innocent unborn *and* the innocent women and children who are victims of domestic violence.

> LET US ADVOCATE FOR THE INNOCENT: THE INNOCENT UNBORN *AND* THE INNOCENT WOMEN AND CHILDREN WHO ARE VICTIMS OF DOMESTIC VIOLENCE.

We must acknowledge that domestic violence is a sin and a crime. It is a wrong mindset and a wrong heart attitude on the part of the abuser.

An abused woman who is a Christian will generally seek help first from pastors and women leaders.[30] These two groups especially need to receive education and training as the dynamics of abuse are complicated. LifeWay Research found 52% of senior pastors don't have enough training to address cases of domestic violence.[31] How can we serve our congregations and protect our flock when we are underprepared to minister and counsel in a situation that can cost lives?

As ministry leaders, we need to respect the courage exhibited and the risks taken by a woman sharing her story. Her secret has been shrouded in humiliation, misplaced guilt, and fear–always the fear: fear she will not be believed (victim shaming), fear she will be told why it's her fault (victim blaming), and fear her abuser will find out and retaliate. If she is returning home after seeking counsel, understand that she has risked additional harm by disclosing her abuse. She is seeking help with the hope that her church family will step in with love and mercy. Accept her assessment of danger as accurate and respect her strategies for mitigating risks.[32]

Hoodwinked

The first step in helping take back our families is admitting that we have been lied to and deceived. We must recognize that abusers have influenced even the most astute professionals. They can appear to be repentant and self-controlled but are quite manipulative and dangerous. Their public behavior and private behavior are incongruous. Despite their controlled grip on the relationships around them, they must be willing to be accountable for their behavior and accept responsibility for their abuse. [33]

How do we begin to make a difference? We can get to know the professionals and resources in our community. We can ensure that church members know that their church leadership is a safe place where their fears will be acknowledged. We can know how to assess risk for victims and their families. We can create a safety plan for victims who stay or plan to leave.

What the Faith Community Can Do[34]

1. Let your voice be heard. Let your congregation know that you have zero tolerance for abuse.

2. Educate your congregations. Routinely speak from the pulpit and write articles about violence in the home. Display posters, brochures, and local/national resource information.

3. Encourage and support training and education for clergy, lay leaders, chaplains, and seminary students.

4. Lead by example. Become involved: volunteer at a shelter, serve as a board member, receive training to become a crisis volunteer.

5. Become a safe haven for women and children.

6. Intervene if you suspect violence is occurring in a relationship, making sure to talk to each person separately. Help create safety plans and use risk assessments to determine the level of danger present.

7. Offer facilities for training and support groups. Serve as a safe place for supervised visits.

8. Partner with existing programs or provide help for individuals.

9. Address internal allegations of abuse and beliefs that foster abuse.

10. Make, distribute, and enforce a policy statement regarding abuse. For example: "...we have not wavered in our belief that churches and their leaders are essential—life-giving and spirit-empowering—components in any community-based response to domestic violence. We believe that most Christian people, when provided with both biblical teaching condemning violence and social-science data about its consequences, will want to do something about it. We do not believe the spirit-filled life should include abusive acts, nor should it turn a blind eye to the suffering of another."[35]

Let Us Proclaim

"We are communities of peace.

We will not be bystanders to violence.

We will be a community of mutuality, supporting the victims of abuse and their children while holding the abusers accountable for their abusive behavior and beliefs.

We will be life-affirming and life-saving in all our actions."

Jeanne Meurer FSM[36]

Chapter 2

The Myths of Abuse

Love is patient and kind; love does not envy or boast; it is not arrogant or rude. It does not insist on its own way; it is not irritable or resentful; it does not rejoice at wrongdoing, but rejoices with the truth. Love bears all things, believes all things, hopes all things, endures all things. I Corinthians 13:4-7 ESV

How much do you know about domestic violence? Without understanding the dynamics of domestic violence, an onlooker may be quick to judge erroneously. You must understand the amount of fear, intimidation, and manipulation to which victims are subjected. If you don't know exactly the type of abuse and manipulation she is dealing with, it can be difficult to understand why someone in an abused relationship chooses to stay. Domestic violence is more than just broken bones and bruises. If you have never been a victim of domestic violence, then thank God! But since it can be difficult for people in healthy relationships to understand what this abuse really looks like, let's look at some of the common myths and facts about something that affects so many people, every single day.

Myth: *Domestic violence is a private family matter.*

Some people say that what happens at home, should stay at home. Domestic violence isn't the same as complaining that your spouse leaves his socks next to the hamper instead of in it. We have to stop comparing normal marital quarrels with something that endangers someone's life. Abuse is everyone's business. Keeping domestic violence a secret helps no one. The harm to children is well documented. Additionally, consider the substantial costs to society and the consequences of perpetuating abuse through learned patterns of behavior. Are we prepared to clean up the generational damage done by perpetuating the need to keep the home life "at home"?

Myth: *Most of the time, domestic violence is not really that serious.*

Domestic violence is an illegal act in the US and is considered a crime with serious repercussions. The definition of domestic violence lacks the ability to cover all of the ways that someone suffering will be abused. The other detrimental aspects of domestic violence (e.g., emotional, psychological, spiritual abuse) may not be considered criminal in a legal sense, but these hidden aspects of abuse can, and often do, result in serious and long-term harm. Every single act of domestic violence needs to be taken seriously.

Myth: *Victims provoke their partners' violence.*

No one deserves to be harmed. Ever. We can never truly gauge what is going on in another's life. To say that anyone deserves to be abused by a spouse or partner based on the victim's behavior shows how little we understand of the true meanings of abuse. Whatever problems exist in a relationship, the use of violence is never justifiable or acceptable. There is NO EXCUSE for domestic violence.

Myth: *Domestic violence is an impulse control or anger management problem.*

There are plenty of people who would like to use mental disorders and anger issues as a way to negate and excuse the behavior of others. Usually, these are people close to the abuser. Admitting that a brother, a son, or a father is an abuser can be difficult. The truth of the matter is that abusers choose whom to abuse and act deliberately and with forethought. For example, an abuser will selectively batter his wife but not his boss. Those who are truly battling an anger issue unrelated to domestic violence will be unable to control their anger toward others, no matter who they might be. They won't specifically target their significant other.

Myth: *No one would beat his pregnant wife or girlfriend.*

Research has shown that pregnancy and childbirth can bring rapid escalations to violence and abuse. Unfortunately, homicide is the single most frequent cause of maternal death during pregnancy and in the first year after giving birth. When we have information that supports a deeper need to protect the sanctity of all life, how can we continue to allow harm to go unanswered?

Myth: *Women are just as violent as men in relationships.*

This is bold statement, and one that needs to be addressed. Men are generally stronger and bigger than women. While some women report striking their male partners during conflict, it is often in self-defense. This false claim of women being the aggressor becomes an excuse by the abuser for the justification of his violence. Statistically, women rarely commit deliberate acts that result in fear, injury, rape, or death.

Myth: *Domestic violence is bad, but it isn't happening everywhere. It doesn't happen in my community, my neighborhood, my culture, my religion, or my congregation.*

Domestic violence doesn't have favorites. It isn't something that just happens during hard times to families that are struggling financially. It happens to people of every educational and socio-economic level. Domestic violence happens in all races, religions, and age groups. It occurs in both heterosexual and same-sex relationships. We have to eliminate the misconceptions concerning what an abusive situation looks like so that families who do not fit the stereotypes are not over-looked for help.

Myth: *Children generally are neither aware of, nor affected by, their mothers' abuse.*

Nearly 90% of children who live in homes in which there is domestic violence will see or hear the abuse. We are impacted by what we experience. Even young children bear the marks of witnessing abuse. Many will have recurring nightmares or relive memories that come flooding back as if they are experiencing them all over again. Children as young as toddlers can suffer from the effects of exposure to abuse. Children exposed to violence and other forms of trauma may have permanent alterations in brain structure, chemistry, and function. This physical change in the brain is just another important reason to address abuse as early as possible to help prevent even further damage.

Myth: *Domestic violence can affect older women, but it is quite rare.*

Abuse doesn't necessarily decrease with age. Approximately half of all elder abuse involving women is thought to be domestic violence "grown old." Since, for many years, the church was completely removed from stepping in to protect domestic violence victims, many women stayed indefinitely because they believed it to be their only option. The stance of the church against divorce and the responsibility placed on women to make the marriage work kept many of our previous generations trapped in a permanent cycle of abuse. Tragically, older battered women are less likely to seek and receive help.

Myth: *Anger management programs are briefer, more cost effective than, and just as successful as certified batterer intervention programs.*

Programs designed to overcome anger problems deal with recognizing, understanding, and adjusting responses to stressful, emotionally-charged situations. Programs focusing on abusive behavior allow time to examine underlying issues for the need to exert control over victims. Battering is a choice founded in the abuser's deep-seated core values and beliefs, not sudden angry outbursts. The goal of anger management programs is to prevent, diffuse, or redirect anger. The goal of batterer intervention programs is victim safety.

Myth: *Since domestic violence is a problem in the relationship, marriage or couple-focused pastoral counseling is key to restoring tranquility in the family or relationship.*

All types of couples counseling comes with increased risk to the victim. Many abusers are charming, believable, and manipulative. If an abuser also happens to display borderline or narcissistic personality characteristics, therapists, counselors, law enforcement, court personnel, and even pastors can be manipulated into believing the batterer's version of the truth. In counseling sessions, he often blames the victim, denies her allegations, and minimizes the severity of the situation. This often increases the risk of violence to the victim, especially after sessions. Faith and religious community representatives can promote safety and restore personal integrity and self-esteem to the victim by suggesting batterer intervention services for the abuser. For the safety of the family, clergy and pastoral leadership should not engage in couples counseling unless the long-term safety of the survivor and of staff can be assured. Abusers see outside help as undermining the control they have created, and retaliation can be dangerous for everyone involved.

Myth: *Services for victims are staffed by people angry at traditional society who want to break up the family unit.*

The goal of counseling and other survivor services is not to break up the family unit but to preserve the safety of all its members. Programs that help battered women and their children and counselors who provide assistance are concerned first and foremost with the safety of the survivor and her dependent children. The goal is never sabotaging family relationships. But, the truth is, sometimes safety and well-being come at the cost of leaving something dangerous and damaging. Achieving this goal, unfortunately, may mean that some relationships need to end.

Myth: *It is easy for a victim to leave her abuser, so if she doesn't leave, it means she likes the abuse or is exaggerating how bad it is.*

Especially within the Church where love and hope should abound, this is the most toxic and detrimental myth that victims face. Fear, lack of safe options, and inability to survive economically prevent many women from leaving abusive relationships. Additionally, emotional gaslighting that convinces the victims they could never make it on their own and threats of harm, including death to the victim and/or children, keep many battered women trapped in abusive situations. Sadly, keeping the status quo in the abusive relationship is often safer for women. The most dangerous time for a battered woman is when she attempts to leave her abuser. When the status quo changes, the danger increases even more. When the abuser discovers that she has made plans to leave, her life and the life of her children could very much be at risk.[37]

WE, AS THE CHURCH, HAVE THE POWER TO BRING HOPE, SAFETY, AND STRENGTH.

These are just a few of the many myths that misrepresent domestic violence victims each day. They stay quiet in their hopelessness because they have been shown by not only society but by the Church that being believed and finding support is difficult. We, as the Church, have the power to bring hope, safety, and strength to those who have been made to believe they are less than God's masterpiece. Christ died for all. The Church must stand up for the sanctity of all life. It's time for the Church to place more value on the sanctity of life than on the sanctity of marriage.

Chapter 3

What is Domestic Violence?

The Lord tests the righteous, but His soul hates the wicked and the one who loves violence. Psalm 11:5 ESV

"Domestic violence is a pattern of assaultive and coercive behaviors, including physical, sexual, and psychological attacks, as well as economic coercion, that adults or adolescents use to gain power and control over their intimate partners."[38]

The act of love is to say, "I want you to be who you are."
The act of abuse is to say, "I want you to be who I want you to be."
It is that simple.
~ James D. Gill

If I asked you to write down the definition of domestic violence, what key items would you include? It is a common misconception that abusers are just angry and lacking self-control. The truth is domestic violence is not about anger but the power and control of another person through fear, manipulation, and intimidation. It is not about impulsive, out-of-control behavior but more purposeful, deliberate actions of the abuser toward his victim. It is a choice. It is a sin.[39]

Truly, all relationships have problems, but domestic violence relationships are not typical relationships subject to typical problems. The problem is not just a "lover's spat," "marital problems," "a private matter," or a "couple's quarrel." Despite the negative conditioning that many in domestic violence situations face, it is not about one partner simply failing to meet the needs of the other partner. It is about unrealistic, unfair, and intentionally ever-changing expectations. Abusive intimate partner relationships suffer from a gross inequity of power. The results are the domination and oppression of the weaker partner. The abuser uses proven tactics of fear, intimidation, isolation, and manipulation to attack his victim. Imagine having your freedoms stripped away, your financial resources out of reach, and your personal choices limited. Imagine nonexistent free will, restricted relationships, and negated emotions.

WHETHER THE WOMAN RESPONDS BY FIGHTING BACK (FIGHT RESPONSE), FLEEING (FLIGHT RESPONSE), SHUTTING DOWN (FREEZE RESPONSE), OR COMPLYING (FAWN RESPONSE), ALL ARE NATURAL AND NORMAL RESPONSES TO AN INTENSELY THREATENING SITUATION.

Scientific evidence shows when we are in fear mode we are caught in a cycle of neurological and chemical responses that dictate the choices we make and the reactions we trigger. In fear mode, we are at the mercy of our circumstances, our body, and our toxic past memories. Our true selves vanish.[40]

Think of fear mode as our survival mode. It is easy to become overwhelmed by what is happening to a point where every response is one of preservation and compliance. Whether the woman responds by fighting back (fight response), fleeing (flight response), shutting down (freeze response), or complying (fawn response), all are natural and normal responses to an intensely threatening situation.

It is difficult for someone who has not experienced this kind of abuse to understand why a victim doesn't see what her abuser is doing and confront him or, more importantly, leave. All relationships are complicated, and a relationship with domestic violence as a component is tremendously complicated. Many people will struggle to understand that the victim is not weak, lazy, crazy, or stupid. She is more likely afraid, confused, ashamed, and embarrassed. She herself may not know why she stays. She is doing the best she can to juggle the pressures of everyday life, possibly a family and a job, and living with an abusive partner. The longer she has been in her situation, the more alert to his every action, tone of voice, and change in body language she becomes. Each day demands living in a state of hypervigilance. She is trying to make sense of a senseless situation, trying vainly to figure out what is wrong so it can be fixed. It is demanding, exhausting, and many times it feels hopeless. It is also impossible for her to correct. Only the abuser has the power to stop the abuse.

Victim: I realized I felt like those combat soldiers living in a war zone where they constantly have to be alert to the possible attack of an enemy on any front at any time. For me, every sound, every word, every action was a potential sign of a coming attack. I lived in fear virtually all the time. I was almost always exhausted. Unlike those soldiers, I didn't get R and R [rest and relaxation].

Dynamics of Abuse

Abusers don't start out abusing. As with many others forms of abuse, domestic violence starts with grooming. Grooming isn't just for the victim. Abusers will groom the family as well. Grooming can begin with intense romance and overwhelming attention, sweet words, and gifts. These actions are intended to make future victims close their eyes to the red flags that can pop up. They can be quite charming, kind, charismatic, and attentive. It is only after a period of time, occurring in stages, that their need for power and control surfaces.

How it Begins

The first predatory tactic is to build a deep emotional connection by creating dependence and trust. As the relationship grows, romantic gestures can abruptly turn into intimidation. Abusers typically blame their partners for misunderstanding them or will gaslight to convince the victim they remember things wrong. Despite stress and abuse, victims will work hard to appease the abuser, trying to keep themselves safe and get back to the earlier romantic stage.

The entire coercive process is about breaking down who she is and destroying her old identity by replacing her beliefs, values, and ideas with his. This creates the perfect environment for establishing guilt by shifting responsibility from the abuser to the victim or justifying abusive behavior by blaming the victim. After that, it is easy to make the victim believe the abuse was a punishment, one that was deserved.

Shame and humiliation follow, eroding her confidence and sense of self-worth. "It is all my fault. If I was just a better girlfriend/wife maybe he wouldn't get so angry." She begins to internalize the message that she is bad. The domino effect begins as she withdraws from friends and family, isolating herself and becoming more dependent on her abuser. She shifts from taking care of her needs to trying to be "better" to please him. As time progresses, she gets more and more confused and disoriented by his warped version of reality.

As the fighting and violence accelerates, so does the gaslighting in which his memory of a fight is never the same as hers. She begins to wonder if she is crazy. She may feel anxious or depressed, and as the increased cortisol takes its toll, her stress leads her to a sense of hopelessness and helplessness. She is exhausted and her ability to think and reason are noticeably compromised. Daily tasks become overwhelming.

To keep her in line, he will be kind, falsely apologize for a bad day, and create a false sense of hope. She will be disproportionately grateful for any act of kindness from him, no matter how small, because of her distorted view of reality. She is led by his deceitful behavior to try even harder to please him, hoping the kindness will occur more often. Unfortunately, he will revert to his unpredictable behavior, being kind one day and violent the next. As the abuse continues, she experiences more stress and anxiety. She begins to agree with his criticisms, and in turn attempts to remove any part of her that displeases the abuser. She becomes willing to do or say anything to create moments of kindness and perceived love.

Without realizing it, she begins to think he is right–she is the problem–even though she doesn't know what she has done wrong. She feels guilty about her previous identity and beliefs and begins adopting his way of thinking, abandoning her own in attempts to be a better partner. As time goes on, friends and family may even struggle to recognize her.[41]

Domestic violence is more than just bad days, angry outbursts, and black eyes. The coercive persuasion of the abuser results in months to years to decades of brainwashing the victim. Tragically, it can take years after leaving the abusive situation for her to give up these distorted beliefs. It can be a long journey through the evils of this world to reach a place of light and hope and freedom. We, as the entire church body, can do better. All people, not just our congregations, should expect to find in Christ's church the true help they need to escape the horrors of abuse. We need to choose to stand up and do better.

Chapter 4

Abuse Doesn't Always Leave Bruises: Understanding Emotional and Financial Abuse

The words of a good person give life,
like a fountain of water, but the words of the wicked
contain nothing but violence. Proverbs 10:11 NCV

Contrary to Hollywood's portrayal of abuse on-screen, there are more ways to wound someone than to hit them. Abusers have many different ways they control their victims. Many tactics lack the physical violence we have come to expect. The four main types of abuse are emotional (sometimes called verbal or psychological abuse), physical, sexual, and economic/financial.

Emotional Abuse

The Bible talks about the power of words: they can be a fountain of life or bring great suffering, they can bring life or death, they can build up or tear down,

Death and life are in the power of the tongue, And those who love it will eat its fruit. Proverbs 18:21 NKJV

Do not let any unwholesome talk come out of your mouths, but only what is helpful for building others up according to their needs, that it may benefit those who listen. Ephesians 4:29 NIV

Domestic violence relationships rarely start off with physical abuse. The first assault in an abusive relationship is often verbal. Verbal assault usually involves yelling or aggressively using words to disarm, offend, or attack someone. As it escalates, it becomes threatening, with an increased risk for physical violence, creating intense fear of imminent danger for the victim. "Over time, verbal assaults become part of a larger pattern of psychological (*emotional*) abuse, subjecting and exposing another person to behavior that may result in psychological trauma, including anxiety, chronic depression, or post-traumatic stress disorder."[42]

The National Coalition Against Domestic Violence reveals the prevalence and destruction caused by emotional abuse:

- 48.4% of women and 48.8% of men have experienced at least one incident of psychologically aggressive behavior by an intimate partner.

- 4 in 10 women and 4 in 10 men have experienced at least one form of coercive control by an intimate partner in their lifetime.

- 17.9% of women have experienced a situation in which an intimate partner tried to keep them from seeing family and friends.

- 18.7% of women have experienced threats of physical harm by an intimate partner.

- 95% of men who physically abuse their intimate partners also psychologically abuse them.

- Women who earn 65% or more of their households' income are more likely to be psychologically abused than women who earn less than 65% of their households' income.

- 7 out of 10 psychologically abused women display symptoms of PTSD and/or depression.

- Women experiencing psychological abuse are significantly more likely to report poor physical and mental health and to have more than 5 physician visits in the last year.

- Psychological abuse is a stronger predictor of PTSD than physical abuse among women.[43]

Emotional abuse is hurtful; attacks the character, physical appearance, and abilities/lack of abilities of the victim; may be in the guise of concern or help; is controlling and manipulative; disrespects, disregards, and devalues the victim; appears unpredictable; may send double messages where words and actions don't line up; frequently escalates over time, occurring more often and with more intensity; often accompanies or leads to other types of abuse.

> *The Lord sees what happens everywhere;*
> *he is watching us, whether we do good or evil.*
> *Kind words bring life, but cruel words crush your spirit.*
> *Proverbs 15:3-4 GNT*

Men who verbally abuse use a variety of tactics:

- Belittling the victim by invalidating her opinions or feelings, noting her concerns or accomplishments as insignificant, and using patronizing put-downs

- Countering and correcting to shut down discussions and oppose/deny the victim's reality

- Abusive joking that often refer to a woman's gender, to her mental abilities, or to her competency

- Holding out by refusing to communicate, ignoring or refusing to listen to her, and refusing to share information
- Side-tracking/shutting down to force discussions off track, stop the discussion, or change the subject often by starting to accuse and blame the victim
- Transferring blame for their anger, irritation, or insecurity to the victim
- Faultfinding and criticism veiled as help or advice
- Intimidation through words or actions that imply harm or loss
- Insulting and labeling using demeaning terms
- Exhibiting selective memory by conveniently "forgetting," altering facts, denying/twisting/rewriting reality
- Commanding/demanding instead of respectfully requesting
- Lashing out in angry verbal attacks, yelling, raging, and temper tantrums[44]

Abusers frequently call their partners degrading names, break promises, and accuse them of having affairs. He may compliment her profusely in public and berate her in private. He may humiliate her in public and private. He may threaten to contact her workplace and tell lies about her. He may reveal her personal information to others. He may lie to her family and friends about her and deny his own actions. His actions do not match his words. He sees his partner as the adversary. He is adept at letting everyone know and feel his emotions. He is an expert at dishing out guilt. Victims are constantly trying to figure out what they did wrong and how they can fix it. Even things that are his fault became her fault, a technique sometimes called "flipping the script." Victims are kept on a roller coaster of emotions by abusers as a deliberate tactic to keep them under control.

Victim: I was in an abusive marriage for a number of years. Almost every discussion that entailed any problem resulted in me being at fault or him dismissing the severity of his error. Conversations focused on him: his needs, his plans, his opinions. I couldn't rely on him. He conveniently "forgot" to be available or would claim that I never told him I needed him. I was accused of sleeping with a multitude of men. I was called awful, demeaning names. He belittled my character and my faith. His rage was palpable. I was so terrified of my abuser that even when he called from hundreds of miles away to verbally abuse me, accuse me, and threaten me, I was paralyzed with fear. In reality, he could not physically harm me from so far away but my ability to recognize that truth was nonexistent. Even after leaving the relationship well over a decade ago, the sound of his voice, even if he's on the phone with others, still causes me to be uncomfortable though there may be many miles between us.

"His speech is smooth as butter, yet war is in his heart; his words are more soothing than oil, yet they are drawn swords." Psalm 55:21 NIV

Phrases women who are emotionally abused might hear are sadly common and numerous:

- It's all your fault.
- You're just trying to pick a fight.
- If you weren't so…
- Why can't you just…
- I don't know what you're talking about.
- You can't take a joke.
- You're too sensitive.
- You don't know what you're talking about.
- You're making a big deal out of nothing.
- You always have to have something to complain about.
- I never said that.
- You're a liar.

- You're making that up.

- You think you're so…

- It's none of your business.

- That never happened.

- You think I don't know what you're doing?

- You're crazy!

- Shut the f*** up!

The wounds from domestic violence are not always physical, and the silent scars sometimes take longest to fade. Shifting the thinking of the world around what domestic violence looks like or "should" look like is necessary. According to the US Dept. of Justice, 80% of victims do not present with physical scars. Despite this, we concentrate on the 20% because we are a visual people—if I don't see your pain, your pain does not exist. However, if you turn victims inside out, you will see all the hidden scars they carry. Every 9 to 15 seconds a woman is physically assaulted or killed. Unfortunately, we don't concentrate on the many other abuses happening every 1-8 seconds, before the assault takes place, because we do not see them as warranting intervention or attention. This is why it can be so difficult for victims without physical injuries from abuse to get the help they deserve.[45]

80% OF VICTIMS DO NOT PRESENT WITH PHYSICAL SCARS.

Let us take a stand to protect those who are being overlooked and abandoned, not only by society, but by the Church because their scars are hidden. Just because we can't see the damage doesn't mean they don't merit our help or attention. We don't have to see their pain to know that it exists.

Then the King will say, "I'm telling the solemn truth: Whenever you did one of these things to someone overlooked or ignored, that was me—you did it to me. Matthew 25:40 MSG

Financial Abuse

Economic abuse may not seem as severe as other types of abuse. The truth is, multiple types of abuse may be happening within each relationship, and each one adds to the emotional and physical distress that a victim feels when trapped in an abusive situation. Financial scarcity often prohibits women from escaping their abuser sooner or at all. Lack of finances can influence her decision to return to the abusive situation. Not having money limits options. Even after leaving, it can take years to restore damaged credit ratings and pay off debts caused by economic abuse.

Economic abuse occurs when someone controls, manipulates, or damages the financial stability of another.

- Between 94-99% of domestic violence survivors have also experienced economic abuse.

- Between 21-60% of victims of domestic violence lose their jobs due to reasons stemming from the abuse.

- Victims of domestic violence lose a total of 8 million days of paid work each year.[46]

Victim: After filing for divorce and the ensuing legal issues following, I missed so many days of work! Meetings with my attorney, his attorney, the prosecutor, the victim advocate plus the civil and criminal court proceedings were necessary, but it was embarrassing having to explain why I had to miss work again. Each time I was praying my pay wouldn't get docked. My job was demanding so it was incredibly stressful trying to prepare for missing work and then trying to catch up afterward each time. The emotional and financial stress definitely took a toll.

Some examples of economic abuse follow:

- rigidly controlling finances, hiding money, withholding money or credit cards
- applying for credit cards, loans, or opening accounts in her name without her consent
- forcing her to take out loans or sign financial documents
- stealing from her or taking her money or wages
- refusing to work, getting fired, or getting her fired
- harassing her at work or school
- making her the sole support of the family
- sabotaging her attempts to work or go to school
- running up debt, ruining her credit rating
- selling her possessions
- disabling vehicles to keep the victim isolated
- making her account for every penny spent, restricting her to an allowance
- withholding basic necessities (food, clothes, shelter, medications)
- refusing her access to community or church financial resources

Abusers often use finances to control their victims. Particularly in patriarchal religious communities, abusive husbands may escape under the radar of detection by appealing to common cultural practices. For instance, it is a valid choice for a woman to decide to be a stay-at-home wife or mother, but this must be her personal decision and free of coercion. Some abusers will force or manipulate their wives (and sometimes daughters) into domestic service, disallowing

THE TACTICS OF MANIPULATION DON'T STOP ONCE A VICTIM HAS LEFT.

them from gaining education or income. This makes it very difficult for a person to leave a dangerous relationship. From the outside, this may appear to be a mutual decision and common Christian practice, but on the inside it can be a cover for financial abuse.[47]

These financial restrictions can make it impossible to leave an abusive partner. Even more troubling, for those who are able to leave, an inability to secure a stable income may force them to return to an abusive partner. Victims of coerced debt may face massive barriers to economic self-sufficiency, including struggling to find a job or even a place to live. The depth of financial consequences that a victim faces may not be fully known until after she leaves her abuser. Finding out the level of debt and its detrimental effects on their personal credit scores can be like the door slamming closed on obtaining their freedom.[48]

The tactics of manipulation don't stop once a victim has left. Often, the abuser will try to lure her back by buying her or the children gifts. He may offer to bring over money or items he knows she needs, intending to woo her back once he gets there. He may pay for fun activities and vacations with the kids that the woman can no longer afford—a tactic meant to persuade her how good it could be for the family if she just reconciles with him. If wooing doesn't work, he may still attempt to control her financially by failing to pay court-ordered child support, medical insurance/bills, car payments, credit card bills, vehicle payments, or mortgages, leaving her to struggle for the most basic needs. She may begin to doubt whether leaving was such a good idea.

Victim: He was court-ordered to pay child support and even agreed to an amount. When the first payment didn't come, I realized he wasn't going to pay. I had so counted on that money because of the debt I had racked up during the lengthy divorce process. I was a successful career woman who couldn't pay for her electricity and water. I had to wait for several months to be able to act because a certain amount of time had to pass or a set threshold of money owed me had to be reached before anyone would help me. He also failed to pay for medical bills and insurance for our child, leading to more stress from bill collectors calling. Because he wouldn't sign the proper paperwork for the transfer of property, I couldn't refinance or sell. I lost our home to foreclosure. Once again, I was abused even though we were no longer married.

According to God's Word, it is the man's responsibility to provide for his family. That doesn't mean women can't help with finances, but God gave the ultimate responsibility of provision to the man. Many abusive men ignore that responsibility.

"But if anyone does not provide for his own,
and especially for those of his household, he has denied
the faith and is worse than an unbeliever." 1 Timothy 5:8 NKJV

Chapter 5

Seen and Unseen Abuse: Understanding Physical and Sexual Abuse

God Most High, have pity on me! Have mercy. I run to you for safety.
In the shadow of your wings, I seek protection till danger dies down.
I pray to you my protector. Psalm 57:1-2 CEV

How plausible is something if you don't have proof? Physical abuse is the most recognized type of abuse. Why? Because we can see it. We have proof that someone has done something wrong, and we can better understand something that isn't invisible. Physical abuse is any physically aggressive behavior, withholding of physical needs, indirect physically harmful behavior, or threat of physical abuse.[49]

According to the National Coalition Against Domestic Violence, physical abuse pervades American society. Consider that more than 10 million Americans are victims of physical violence annually. Ten million is unacceptable. Each of those men and women is someone's son or daughter. Every minute, 20 people are victims of physical violence in the United States. In their lifetime, 1 in 3 women and 1 in

4 men are victims of some form of physical violence by an intimate partner. That means many of our friends and family have experienced intimate partner violence and have either chosen not to share or are still silently battling this abuse alone. Discussions about healthy relationships are vital and need to include our youth and other single persons. A majority of physical abuse is committed by dating partners rather than spouses. Almost half of intimate partner homicides are committed by dating partners. More than 75% of women aged 18-49 struggling with partner violence were previously abused by the same perpetrator.

Tragically, 1 in 7 women and 1 in 18 men are severely injured by intimate partners, and 40% of female murder victims are killed by their intimate partners. Are there any warning signs? Seventy-six percent of those women who were killed and 85% of women who survived homicide attempts were stalked prior to the murder or attempted murder. Only slightly more than half of intimate partner physical violence is ever reported to law enforcement.[50]

Our vision and definition of abuse has been obscured for far too long. Public service announcements and media attention typically focus on physical abuse, perhaps because the evidence of abuse is there in plain sight. The truth is physical abuse does not have to result in bodily harm. The threat or demonstration of harm or endangerment is still physical abuse.

THE THREAT OR DEMONSTRATION OF HARM OR ENDANGERMENT IS STILL PHYSICAL ABUSE.

Although most people associate physical abuse with the use of physical force to injure someone, many physical abusers never strike their partners. However, he can throw things at her, deprive her of sleep, and destroy her things by breaking them or setting them on fire. He could kick in doors or kick out windows. He never hits her– he never has to. The implied threat of what could happen is enough for the woman to do what he wants.

Victim: I thought because he never blacked my eyes or broke any bones that I wasn't physically abused. Whenever he broke my stuff in a drunken fit of rage, I wondered if he would break me next. When he kicked the door off, I was terrified I would be the next target. I was always terrified he would follow through with his angry threats of "I'll f*** you up!" or that he'd carry out his calm descriptions of how easy it is to kill someone and get away with it.

When you try to explain the fear that exists in every aspect of your life to someone who has never experienced it, they just can't comprehend it. They keep looking for the visible signs that you are wounded, but the wounds I am talking about are the ones that cause internal damage done to your body, soul, and spirit. If you have ever experienced that feeling of dread when you feel something bad is going to happen, imagine that feeling hundreds of times worse– all the time. This black cloud, this heaviness, this looming feeling of impending doom is with you 24/7. There is no relief, even when he is gone because his presence lingers.

One night he came home from the bar already enraged. It seemed someone at the bar had hit him with no warning. He had come home in a hurry to get his gun before the bar closed. He expected me to help him find it. Then, when he couldn't find the bullets, he accused me of hiding them. I denied it, which only made him madder. He kicked the dog in his frustration. The fear of what happens next is overwhelming. What should I do? If I tell him where the bullets are, he might go shoot somebody. If I don't tell him where the bullets are, he might shoot me if he finds them after the bar is closed. What would you do?

Below is a list of words and situations typically associated with physical abuse.

- abandoning
- kicking
- spitting

- shaking
- scratching
- twisting

- strangling/choking
- stabbing
- shooting
- burning
- breaking
- throwing
- drowning
- beating
- grabbing
- restraining
- slapping
- pushing/pulling
- tripping
- slamming
- punching
- biting
- hitting
- pinching
- threatening with/use of a weapon
- destroying property
- locking out of residence
- destroying nearby inanimate objects
- abandoning in dangerous places
- denying physical comfort
- withholding food/drink
- refusing to help with medical needs
- driving recklessly
- disrupting sleep
- limiting freedom
- abusing/threatening to abuse children or pets

"The woman who is emotionally abused fears for the loss of herself and sanity, while a woman who is physically abused fears for the loss of herself, sanity, and life."[51]

Sexual Abuse

In any intimate relationship, sex is still something that should be considered consensual. Sadly, many abusers with any biblical knowledge will push sex as a marital duty, using guilt and biblical obedience as a tool to get what they want. "Sexual violence is non-consensual conduct of a sexual nature. It is purposeful, violent behavior. The perpetrator accomplishes sexual violence through threat, coercion, exploitation, deceit, force, physical or mental incapacitation, and/or using power or authority."[52] Sexual abuse is the opposite of what God commands in His word.

So husbands ought to love their own wives as their own bodies; he who loves his wife loves himself. For no one ever hated his own flesh, but nourishes and cherishes it, just as the Lord does the church.
Ephesians 5:28-29 NKJV

Abusers who are physically violent toward their intimate partners are often sexually abusive as well. Victims who are both physically and sexually abused are more likely to be injured or killed than victims who experience a single form of abuse. Abusers assault people of all genders, races, ages, social classes, and ethnicities. Women who are disabled, pregnant, or attempting to leave their abusers are at greatest risk for intimate partner rape.[53]

- Intimate partner sexual assault and rape are used to intimidate, control, and demean victims/survivors of domestic violence.

- Intimate partner sexual assault is more likely to cause physical injury than stranger or acquaintance assault.

- Between 14% and 25% of women are sexually assaulted by intimate partners during their relationship.

- Between 40% and 45% of women in abusive relationships will also be sexually assaulted during the course of the relationship.

- Over half of women raped by an intimate partner were sexually assaulted multiple times by the same partner.

- Women who are sexually abused by intimate partners report more risk factors for intimate partner homicides than non-sexually abused women.

- Women who are sexually abused by intimate partners suffer severe and long-lasting physical and mental health problems, similar to those of other rape victims. They have higher rates of depression and anxiety than women who were either raped by a non-intimate partner or physically but not sexually abused by an intimate partner.[54]

When we look at the reasons behind sexual abuse, we see the similarities to other types of abuse: it's all about his needs, his sense of entitlement, his way to establish power and dominance. His victim ceases to be a person to him. He craves a partner who has no will of her own. A large number of victims report a surprising fact: their abuser doesn't appear interested in sex although he was previously interested. He may have discovered she is not his ideal sexual partner or his physical expectation of a perfect partner. He may be having sex with other partners. At least one-quarter of abusive men cheat on their partners repeatedly. He may choose to live in his sexual fantasy world established as a teenager exposed to pornography. Pornography feeds his belief of entitlement. Pressuring his partner to watch pornography is a way of normalizing his desires. He may be withholding sex as a control tactic. He may have lost his sex drive due to drug or alcohol use. He may be attracted to men. He uses the highs of satisfying sexual experiences and the lows of no sexual activity to keep her off balance.[55]

Sexual abuse encompasses more than being forced or coerced into taking part in unwanted sexual activity. It may be accompanied by or followed by physical violence. It may also include denying the use of contraception or protection against sexually transmitted diseases.

Marriage is to be held in honor among all [that is, regarded as something of great value], and the marriage bed undefiled [by immorality or by any sexual sin]; for God will judge the sexually immoral and adulterous. Hebrews 13:4 AMP

"What happens in the bedroom is so personal and private between a couple that sexual abuse often may not be discussed when reporting other abuse. In a Texas study, nearly 70% of women seeking orders of protection were raped. In Massachusetts 55% were sexually assaulted by their abusers but none included this information on her statement. In Colorado, only 4 percent of women listed forced sex on the complaint form requesting the temporary restraining order."[56]

Victims may not discuss what happened to them sexually for a long time because it can be so humiliating and degrading to talk about. They also may be trying to understand how the person who is supposed to love and cherish them could treat them so badly. Ongoing sexual abuse discounts her needs and reinforces his damaging treatment of her. It is often the last type of abuse to which a victim will admit. A true sense of trust, acceptance, and freedom from judgment must be in place before victims feel comfortable enough to share something so personal.

Victim: As my awareness of what was happening to me grew, so did my instinct to distance myself. Every act of intimacy left me ashamed and crying alone in my bathroom. The last time I ever let him touch me was after a concert. He got home super late, and our three daughters were asleep in our bed. He woke me up to "talk" in the living room. His talk was just his attempt at intimacy. I told him I wasn't feeling well, and that I just wanted to get back to snuggling with the girls. He belittled me for not living up to my biblical duty to submit to him as the Bible required me as his wife. I didn't have enough biblical knowledge to feel anything other than defeated. It was the last time I would let him put his hands on me. Later, he told me that had he known that was the last time we would have sex, he would have made it more worth his while. I shudder to think what more I might have endured.

We have created a culture in which marital sexual abuse is acceptable and justified. With only 36% of all rape victims ever reporting the crime to the police, the percentage of married women reporting spousal rape to the police is even lower. Marital rape is the most underreported form of sexual assault. When spousal rape happens in a home with children, 18% of female victims say their children witnessed the crime. The staggering statistical chance of between 10%-14% of married women being raped at some point during their marriages should put us at high alert. Not just in the community, but as leaders in the Church, it is our responsibility to ensure we are not supporting a marital culture in which spousal rape is accepted or tolerated.

The sad truth is that until 1976, state laws specifically exempted spousal rape from general rape laws. Think about that. Rape was legal if you were married. In 1976, Nebraska was the first state to legally recognize nonconsensual intercourse with a spouse as rape. By 1993, all 50 states had either completely or partially repealed their spousal rape exemptions. However, even now, some states still have some form of spousal rape exemptions, and it is often legally considered a different, lesser crime than non-spousal rape. Tragically, despite changing laws to create better accountability for abusers, many Americans do not believe marital rape is actually rape.[57]

MANY AMERICANS DO NOT BELIEVE MARITAL RAPE IS ACTUALLY RAPE.

We need to acknowledge that sexual abuse happens in marriages as well as in other intimate partner relationships. We need to change the current viewpoint that spouses have fewer rights than an unmarried partner. Wives have a legal right to say "NO!" Consent is based on choice. In relationships with domestic violence, there is an imbalance of power. Giving in because of fear or pressure or threats is not consent. Giving in because her partner will wear her down until she does is really forcing her. If a woman cannot safely say "no," then her "yes" has no meaning.

Marriage was created by God and was meant to be based on trust, mutual intimacy, adoration, devotion, respect, and commitment. Sexual abuse and marital rape destroy trust and degrade what is meant to be holy. At the hands of an abuser, what God intends as marital intimacy between partners, turns mutual pleasure into torment and degradation. The abuser's sense of entitlement and ownership reduces his partner to an object, a possession for his pleasure.

He may constantly pressure her to engage in sex and threaten or hurt her for refusing. No tenderness is shown. There is no right to consent. Sex is not something to be taken, forced, demanded, or coerced. It is not something to be demanded out of a sense of entitlement, but it is to be freely enjoyed as a mutual expression of love and desire.

> THE ABUSER'S SENSE OF ENTITLEMENT AND OWNERSHIP REDUCES HIS PARTNER TO AN OBJECT, A POSSESSION FOR HIS PLEASURE.

The following are signs of sexual coercion:

- continuing to pressure the woman after she has said "No"
- giving extravagant compliments in an attempt to get her to agree to sex encounters
- giving drugs or alcohol to "loosen up" her inhibitions
- insisting she dress in a more sexual way than she wants
- forcing her to remain naked
- coercing her into sexual acts she is uncomfortable with, such as sex with a third party, physically painful sex, or activities she finds offensive or degrading
- inflicting sex-specific injuries
- expecting sex as a way to "prove her love"
- reacting with anger, resentment, or sadness if she refuses to do what he wants
- creating fear of what will happen if she doesn't agree to have sex
- normalizing his need "as a man" to have sex

- making her feel obligated to have sex
- threatening to go somewhere else for sex

Victim: He would come in drunk expecting to have sex. I would have been in bed for hours because I had to be at work in the morning. It never worked to try and pretend to be asleep. He would just turn on the lights, rip the covers off me, turn up the radio, or shake the bed. Sometimes it was more than one of them. If I tried to resist, I was told he should just have stayed at the bar. There were plenty of women there he could have sex with. Then he would try again to initiate sex. I knew from past history he would just keep pressuring me until he got what he wanted. If I wanted to get any sleep at all, I had to submit. I would pray, "God, please let him hurry up and pass out." I distinctly remember being torn and cleaning myself up in the bathroom in the dark with tears streaming down my face as he slept.

"Husbands, love your wives [seek the highest good for her and surround her with a caring, unselfish love], just as Christ also loved the church and gave Himself up for her." *Ephesians 5:25 AMP*

Domestic violence is a worldwide crisis, and we each have a responsibility to lift our voices on behalf of the victims so they know they are not alone. God counts their tears, and we can be a safe place for these suffering children of God. They need to feel assured that they can seek refuge with us. When it comes to sexual abuse in marriage, the Church and its leaders have been quiet for far too long. It is time to speak up against what our congregations are experiencing in their homes. Christ called us to serve the hurting. As a leader in ministry, you become an accessory in these crimes when you dismiss them as being within biblical rights. We need to ask ourselves the hard question: "If someone came to you for help, with or without visible wounds, seeking safety and solace, would you answer the call?"

Chapter 6

Who Are the Abused?

Do you not know that you are the temple of God and that the Spirit of God dwells in you? I Corinthians 3:16 NKJV

Stereotyping happens in every area of life and domestic violence is no stranger to it. If you asked 10 of your friends who they thought were more likely to be abused, what kind of answers do you think you would get?

"Anyone can be a victim of domestic violence. There is NO "typical victim." Victims of domestic violence come from all walks of life, varying age groups, all backgrounds, all communities, all education levels, all economic levels, all cultures, all ethnicities, all religions, all abilities and all lifestyles."[58]

Domestic violence is the leading cause of injury to women—more than car accidents, muggings, and rapes combined.[59] These women are victims of a crime. They aren't going crazy; they are having a normal reaction to a crazy situation. They are survivors with strengths, courage, and skills that have allowed them to survive this far. They are women deserving of support from family, friends, the community, and the Church.

You know abused women. Those victimized are your mother, sister, daughter, niece, friend, neighbor, or co-worker. Many women who have not yet shared their story are searching for a person they feel is safe, who will not judge, deny, or minimize what is being related. They may have reached out for help before and gotten a response that was not what they needed at that time.

> A battered woman may not be an expert concerning her own situation. In fact, because she is trapped in an unpredictable relationship in which she experiences the high of true love one moment and the depths of sadness and hurt the next, a battered woman can be like a ship tossed helplessly by the waves. She may have difficulty realizing her predicament because, in order to survive her circumstances, she doesn't listen to or trust her own instincts…She may not realize she needs help or support, and denies the danger of her position. Furthermore, she may not even comprehend that there are people out there who can furnish a sense of stability and acceptance.[60]

"Many women feel like failures because they have not stopped the man they love from psychologically abusing and controlling them… saying: 'I let it happen' and 'I feel like I've failed'… Women describe feeling emotionally beaten down, shame, guilt, anger, sadness, depression, lack of confidence, insecure, discouraged, defeated, desperate, fearful, anxious and full of dread. They talk about being codependent, having self-doubt, a low belief in their abilities, confused, a feeling of going insane and an inability to concentrate."[61]

She may appear happy, calm, and confident. She may appear angry, defensive, and rebellious. She may appear helpless, depressed, and exhausted. She may keep herself distant, controlled, withdrawn from others or appear clingy, anxious, and needy. Regardless of how she presents herself, she is experiencing great inner turmoil during a large part of her abusive relationship. She is preoccupied with wondering how to please him and how to get him to change, often to the detriment of her own well-being and that of her children.

Women who are emotionally abused largely exhibit the same anguish as women who have been physically battered.[62] She may be reluctant to disclose her abuse because she fears no one will believe her. She may have shared her story with someone she trusts, only to have that her experiences rejected or minimized. She may have been judged for staying with or returning to her abuser. Even more debilitating is the unsolicited advice from the inexperienced. Fear is the root cause of all of her decisions. She is afraid someone will take unwanted action in an attempt to save her. She worries if someone finds out and rejects her, she will be even more isolated and alone. Her biggest fear? Harm coming to whomever she shares her story with and further harm to her or her children.

Add to those fears, the feelings that she has for her abuser. Remember, they started this relationship as one of romance and love. Those feelings don't go away when subtle abuse starts. They become conflicted and confused. She will feel sorry for him when he seems low. On the good days, she can feel loved and flattered. When he has bad days, she can feel responsible and even deserving of the abuse. Through it all, there is a feeling of obligation to stay. She fears ending the relationship, unsure of her safety and future. In his brokenness, she may think she is the only one who can help, that no one else understands him. Deep down, she harbors the hope he will somehow change.

These are women who just want to be in a loving relationship. They want back that charming guy they married who has changed into this abuser gradually over time. He is not always the terrifying Mr. Hyde; sometimes he is the nice Dr. Jekyll.

"It's important to remember that love and intimacy precede the abuse, which can make it difficult to break away. Abusive relationships are not violent all the time. There are periods when a woman is reminded why she fell in love with her partner. Abusers effectively weave together intimacy and abuse to control their partners."[63]

This beloved creation of God is as a hamster on a wheel running around and around, trying to figure out what makes the abuser abuse. She wants to believe her relationship is fixable if she just tries harder, if he quits using drugs, if he gets a different job, if the kids were better behaved, if she/they go to counseling, if the house were nicer/cleaner, if she lost weight. The list of unhealthy and the erroneous beliefs is unending. The average victim will leave yet return to her abuser an average of seven times.[64]

THE AVERAGE VICTIM WILL LEAVE YET RETURN TO HER ABUSER AN AVERAGE OF SEVEN TIMES.

"Many women who apply for a protection order, however, do not follow through with the entire process ... There are a variety of factors that influence women's decisions to follow through with the process to obtain a protection order against their abuser. Zoellner et al. (2000), for example, found that emotional attachment to her partner was an important factor in determining a woman's persistence in the protection order process. Women who reported loving their partner or believing their partner was capable of change were less likely to follow through with the process."[65]

Victim: I was staying with a family from church when he finally convinced me to come back home. I'd been gone for weeks, and he said he realized how much he loved me and really wanted to make our marriage work. He made promises I sincerely thought he would keep this time. My host family advised me not to go, but I assured them this time would be different. They knew I had left several times before and shared their concerns for my safety as I left. At first, things were fine. He was very pleased I was home and treated me well. It wasn't long before I knew I had made a huge mistake. I felt the tension building again and knew the abuse was coming. He had manipulated me once again into believing his lies. Now I was too embarrassed to reach out to my friends who had tried to warn me not to go back.

"In many cases, victims of intimate partner violence try to convince themselves that the domestic violence that they have experienced was a one-time event, and that their partner will not subject them to physical violence again. However, research indicates that physical violence, psychological abuse, sexual abuse, and economic abuse are repetitive patterns."[66] An abused woman hopes things will get better, remains focused on his good points, makes excuses for his abuse, and minimizes what really is happening.

Victim: My mom tried to talk to me about how my abuser was treating me while we went on vacation together for a week without him being present. He was calling several times a day to tell me things I needed to do for the business even though he knew I was over 600 miles from home. She would hear him berate me even as I promised to find a way to take care of whatever the issue was. I would defend him to her and say he was a hard worker and just too busy to handle it himself. I would stay behind and try to solve the latest problem while the others enjoyed the beach. The more he called and interrupted the vacation, the more I felt I had to cover for his bad behavior: he was working long hours, he wasn't sleeping well, he didn't like being without me, he was worried, he missed me, he had a bad day and needed to talk. I would tell her I didn't mind his calls and liked being needed. When it was time to head back home, we had to make a substantial detour so I could take care of something for him. My mom was ticked! She pointed out he had ruined every day of the vacation. Although I was embarrassed, I was not ready to see the abuse.

A victim may not be able to admit her relationship may need to end for her safety and the safety of her children. She grasps at every positive thing that happens in the relationship, no matter how small, as a sign that if she just holds on a little longer, everything will be okay. What she fails to recognize is that the small acts of affection or kindness are contrived to keep her emotionally attached to him. Unfortunately, she learns his sweet promises, meant to get her to return, are insincere and short-lived.

As friends and loved ones of victims, it can be easy to want to swoop in and save them from their suffering. If you are ministering to victims of domestic violence, keep in mind that the primary goal is to empower women and encourage self-reliance– not rescue them. Instead of telling her what she should do, discuss what will happen if certain actions are not taken. Avoid taking over and doing things for her that she is able to handle herself, even if you are trying to be helpful and save time. Offer information about appropriate resources. Our help will benefit an abused woman more if we respect her ability to control her own life, make her own decisions, and develop tools to advocate on her own behalf.[67]

We can help victims realize abuse is not okay. We can help them understand abuse is not their fault. We can discuss the types of abuse and the cycle of violence. We can help them learn the differences between healthy and unhealthy relationships. We can help them recognize relationship red flags. We can help them learn to establish and enforce healthy boundaries. We can help them overcome their fear of being alone and/or abandoned. We can help them discover who they are in Christ. We can help them discover and draw closer to the God who loves them unconditionally. To those of you truly seeking to serve in a way that impacts and empowers women, now, more than ever, is the time to stand with those who have been alone in their abuse and suffering for far too long.

Education is the key to helping. Through education, not only the public but our church leaders and congregations can better understand the true depth and nature of domestic violence. We must be churches that can truly help the hurting to heal by reaching out in grace, mercy and love. We want to shine that beacon of safety to those in our congregations that live with abuse. They aren't waiting for us to rescue them. They simply need us to encourage them in seeking the freedom they have already been granted in Christ.

Chapter 7

The Impact of Abuse

The thief comes only to steal and kill and destroy;
I have come that they may have life,
and have it to the full. John 10:10 NIV

Victim: I thought about killing myself more than once throughout the marriage. I read tons of self-help books, listened to all kinds of teachings on marriage, sought counseling, and prayed a lot. No matter what I tried, nothing worked to get things back to what they were before he became abusive. It wasn't that I wanted to die; I just didn't want to live like that anymore. The fear was paralyzing; I wasn't having healthy thoughts. No one knew how desperate I was. Having my daughter changed everything– I stayed alive for her.

> IT WASN'T THAT I WANTED TO DIE; I JUST DIDN'T WANT TO LIVE LIKE THAT ANYMORE.

The impact of abuse on women is immense. Their suffering and pain is immeasurable. They lose their feelings of worth, their confidence, their identity. They lose their inner peace, their faith, their hope. They lose their freedom, security, and safety. They lose their trust, happiness, and friendships. Only through a loving God can they be restored.

According to the Center for Disease Control and Prevention (CDC), "IPV [Intimate Partner Violence] is connected to other forms of violence and causes serious health and economic consequences. Apart from deaths and injuries, physical violence by an intimate partner is associated with a number of adverse health outcomes. Several health conditions associated with IPV may be a direct result of the physical violence. Other conditions are the result of the impact of IPV on the cardiovascular, gastrointestinal, endocrine and immune systems through chronic stress or other mechanisms."[68]

Further, they report, "Health conditions associated with IPV include asthma, bladder and kidney infections, circulatory conditions, cardiovascular disease, fibromyalgia, irritable bowel syndrome, chronic pain syndrome, central nervous system disorders, gastrointestinal disorders, joint disease, migraines and headaches... gynecological disorders, pelvic inflammatory disease, sexual dysfunction, sexually transmitted infections, including HIV/AIDS, delayed prenatal care, preterm delivery, pregnancy difficulties like low birth weight babies and perinatal deaths, unintended pregnancy."[69]

Abuse, no matter what type, affects every part of a victim's life. Their relationships, their health, and their emotional well-being are all at risk. Psychological, sexual, and/or physical abuse can lead to various emotional consequences for victims such as sleep disturbances, low self-esteem, and flashbacks. Then add anxiety and depression, inability to trust and antisocial behavior, fear of intimacy and emotional detachment, and suicidal behavior and symptoms of PTSD (post-traumatic stress disorder). Victims may also engage in high-risk sexual behaviors, use of harmful substances, unhealthy eating behaviors, and overuse of health-related services. The more severe the violence, the greater the correlation to negative health behaviors by victims.[70]

Effects of Domestic Violence on Children

Children are a gift from the Lord;
they are a reward from him. Psalm 127:3 NLT

From an actual conversation between a mother and child after leaving the abusive relationship: "Mom, if Dad kills you, will I have to go live with him?"

"Family violence, whether physical, sexual, emotional, or verbal, is one of the most direct and potentially harmful forms of violence exposure that children experience due to its unique nature. It is usually not a sudden, isolated incident, but rather may involve years of emotional, psychological, and physical trauma that can escalate over time. A child can be an indirect victim of IPV as a witness and still face the serious consequences of the abuse."[71]

Victim: He never raised a hand against my children, but when yelling at me seemed to work less and less, he began bringing them into the battle: calling out my bad behavior by making an example of them, attacking them with his yelling and verbal assaults. They looked on afraid, unsure what was happening. I felt powerless to keep them safe.

The statistics of children facing violence in their homes is staggering. One in 15 children are exposed to intimate partner violence each year, and 90% of these children are eyewitnesses to the abuse.[72] More than 15.5 million US children live in families where partner violence occurred at least once in the past year with 7 million children living in families in which severe partner violence occurred.[73] Knowing that so many children are at risk, we must increase the available safety measures that families need.

Staggering numbers reveal that the majority of US nonfatal intimate partner victimizations of women (two-thirds) occur at home. Forty-three percent of homes experiencing intimate partner violence involving female victims have children present.[74] In a single day in 2007, 13,485 children were living in a domestic violence shelter or transitional housing facility. Another 5,526 sought services at a non-residential program.[75]

Self-reports by mothers who had experienced IPV also revealed that over 40% of their children had been exposed to their IPV victimization.[76] Research suggests an estimated 30% to 60% of the families where domestic violence is identified, some form of concurring child maltreatment is also present.[77] When do we take a stand and say that enough is enough? If we understand that 65% of adults that abuse their partner also physically and/or sexually abuse their children, when will we ensure that the smallest voices are heard?[78] How will we protect future families when research shows that boys who witness domestic violence are twice as likely to abuse their own partners and children when they become adults?[79] Forty-two percent of our youth reporting physical teen violence also report a history of child maltreatment. Two-thirds of those same youth also witnessed an assault between other family members. [80]

In a sample of 100 girls found guilty of delinquent behavior, 69 reported experiencing caregiver violence; 42 reported dating violence; 81 experienced sexual violence; and 90 had witnessed violence.[81] Acting out is just one of the many ways that abuse manifests itself in our youth. While the common answer from those unaffected by abuse is to simply leave, separation does not always protect the children in the relationship. Children may witness more violence in their parents' relationship after separation than before. Sadly, they often become the abuser's target when the adult victim is no longer as accessible.[82]

Victim: My friends always wondered why I was so strict about my daughter's early bedtime, even on the weekends. What they didn't know was I always wanted her to be sound asleep when the abuse happened so she wouldn't see or hear it. I didn't want her to be subjected to his hurtful words and violent actions, so I thought if she was out of his sight, she was out of his mind. It was pretty effective. I was usually able to keep him from waking her up, which made what I was going through a little easier to bear. I didn't want her to be afraid or get hurt. It was my attempt to protect her.

The emotional damage caused when one parent hurts the other often presents as if the child had been the recipient of the abuse. (See Resources 1 and 2) Children who live in homes with domestic violence are deprived of the joys of childhood simply by the disruption of their sense of safety and security. Their well-being, development, and social adjustment are threatened. They may have conflicting emotions about their father whom they both love and fear. They may begin to lose respect for their mother and women in general. Abuse can create a relational disruption impeding the natural establishment or sustaining of nurturing relationships with either parent. They may show no response to the violence in an effort to protect themselves from emotional or physical abuse.

CHILDREN WHO LIVE IN HOMES WITH DOMESTIC VIOLENCE ARE DEPRIVED OF THE JOYS OF CHILDHOOD.

> *Fathers, do not make your children angry,*
> *but raise them with the training*
> *and teaching of the Lord. Ephesians 6:4 NCV*

Children who live in a violent home are at greater risk for abuse and neglect. Those who witness domestic violence are emotionally abused without ever having been physically abused themselves, yet the effects are similar to children who are physically abused. They live in an atmosphere of fear, powerlessness, and helplessness and are forced to bear the burden of protecting the "family secret." Parents are deceived if they believe the children are not aware of what goes on behind closed doors. Children can be affected emotionally, physically, socially, and academically.

Emotional Impact on Children

Emotional effects of abuse on children can result in long-term psychological problems and disorders. Many children living in abusive situations will struggle daily with anxiety and fear. Whether abuse is daily, or more sporadic, it creates a sense of impending doom, one that can interfere with necessary needs for stability and security. As children are exposed to other healthy families, whether at school, church, or even through television and movies, they may wonder why they don't have a functional family. Why do other families get to be happy? Often, this leads to low self-esteem and poor self-concept which can result in depression or misplaced guilt. In order to maintain that everything at home is "okay," children will often isolate and withdraw from their friends, creating more compounded negative effects such as loneliness.

Older children often struggle with reversal of family roles (child becomes caretaker of parents/siblings). Many will take on more of the home burdens to keep siblings safe. The opposite response can also happen and children may use violence and threats to solve problems, especially with siblings. This confusion leads to an inability to trust and the failure to identify and differentiate feelings. Inappropriate responses to different situations have a high probability of leading to shame, self-blame, or guilt.

Children struggling in these situations are often afraid to try something new and typically deal with a fear of abandonment. Many abusers use abandonment as a threat to keep their victims under control. Abandonment fears can lead to difficulty in developing close relationships. Children struggling with such fears often keep relationships at arm's length, sometimes resorting to timidity and shyness. On the other end of the spectrum, some children will have a difficult time understanding personal boundaries.

As with any volatile situation, there is a high probability that children will suffer symptoms that include acting-out behavior, tantrums, development of fantasy worlds, denial/minimizing, and even regressive behaviors (baby talk, phobias, nightmares, etc.).

Victim: A year before I left, my daughters had begun to have night terrors. Walking with their eyes open, hysterical crying, seeing things that weren't there–and worse– my inability to wake them up. A month after we finally got out, my oldest had a night terror that lasted 45 minutes. She cried and told me she didn't want to die. She was wide-eyed, frantic, and inconsolable. Through my own tears, I understood at that moment not only the damage caused to her 8-year-old psyche, but I knew more than ever we had made the right choice to leave. Now I just had to make sure we could stay safe.

Emotions are complicated and that doesn't change just because children are young. In fact, they struggle to understand the way these types of abuses make them feel. Imagine how confusing it must be for a child to look at someone who is meant to love and protect them and who instead inspires in them anger, bitterness, and resentment. The pain of struggling with immense and overwhelming emotional abuse seems impossible to overcome. Fear of abandonment is common. A child can be preoccupied with violence and horror, provocative behavior, and feelings of powerlessness, fear, and helplessness. Love can become associated with violence. All these emotional ramifications can lead to increased risk of suicide.

Physical Effects of Domestic Violence on Children

Even beyond injuries inflicted by an abuser, children victimized by domestic abuse can become more accident prone. Because of constant stress, they are at an increased risk of illness or disease. As with the emotional effects, sleep disturbances can increase, adding more nightmares and night terrors and posing a risk to enuresis/encopresis (bedwetting/soiling). Abuse and neglect puts children at risk and creates higher probability for developmental delays, lapses in memory and a failure to thrive. Stress can often lead to eating disorders and even self-inflicted wounds as children attempt to feel they have something in their life that they can control.

Social Effects of Domestic Violence on Children

When we say children are always watching us, it means that even when we think they can't see or hear, they will still be impacted by our decisions, actions, and words. When children live in a violent home, they may act out at school through aggression and bullying. Children in abusive situations are very likely to self-isolate in an effort to prevent peers from finding out what their home life really looks like. Alcohol and drugs may or may not be present in the home, but kids often numb the pain of their home life through substance use. As the abuse at home increases, so does the probability for delinquent behavior, sexual acting out, risk of being a runaway, and trouble with authority figures. A lack of positive attention at home may often lead to unhealthy needs for attention. Since unhealthy examples are where these needs begin, these increased needs for attention very likely include being violent or verbally abusive toward a dating partner or accepting violence or abuse from a dating partner. This is a vicious cycle as children are at an increased risk to identify with one of their parents and the unhealthy role they play (abuser or victim). This can pass the family violence cycle on to future generations. As this becomes a normal generational occurrence, you will see more and more of this behavior across multiple generations.

Academic Effects of Domestic Violence on Children

Domestic violence affects every area of life. Many children exposed to domestic violence are often affected academically. Abuse often interferes with children's ability to concentrate and reduces their attention span, leading to higher probabilities of academic dysfunction. Abuse in the home can result in excessive/unexplained school absences, partially as a result of frequent moves and school relocations. Many times, children are reluctant to convey somatic (physical) injuries and complaints due to fear of physical repercussions at home. In homes with a lack of parental involvement, children have an increased risk of developmental/language delays and higher incidence of poor academic performance. Without any parental accountability, children may sabotage their own success and struggle with recurrent lost or incomplete homework. They often lack respect for authority, struggle with aggression, and have a higher likelihood of developing aggressive language.

With changes in school performance there can be an increased struggle with hyperactivity, anxiety, and irritability. For students with declining academics, there is a higher probability for lack of involvement in school activities. Even with academically successful children, stress and fear of failure are often the driving forces behind their success. Punishment for lack of achieving often leads a student to perfectionism, overcompliance, and a need to overachieve. Many of these students are often mentally and physically exhausted to the point that they may even fall asleep in class.

"If we want to help children who are exposed to domestic abuse, we have to offer our whole-hearted support to their mothers. We have to give up victim blaming and start understanding the complex realities that abused mothers face. Leaving the abusive man is not a magic answer that immediately brings safety and healing for mothers and children, and we have to be willing to work closely with abused mothers toward viable long-term solutions. We cannot help her children by joining our voices in chorus with his."[83]

Without intervention and specialized treatment to change patterns of thinking and behaving, the generation now living in abuse become the next generation of abusers and victims. "Domestic violence and child abuse are truly 'family violence' exposures that create and maintain a vicious cycle—exposed children are more likely to become involved in IPV throughout adolescence and adulthood as both victims and perpetrators."[84]

To assist an abused woman effectively we have to treat her in a way that is opposite to the abusive man's style. Since he pressures her constantly, we have to be patient. Since he talks down to her, we have to approach her as equals. Since he believes his ideas are superior to hers, we have to draw from her intelligence, rather than assuming we know better than she does on how to improve her circumstances. And since he makes her feel like she's a bad mother, we have to approach her as a good mother, one who is trying hard to figure out how to make life better for her children, and who doesn't need a lecture from us.[85]

Chapter 8

Who Are the Abusers?

For as he thinks in his heart, so is he... Proverbs 23:7 NKJV

Hurt people, hurt people. We have all heard this phrase, and we can all step back from people who have hurt us and recognize where those behaviors may not have had anything to do with us or our actions. That truth also applies to abusers, but on a higher and more severe level. Abusers are emotionally broken, angry, and controlling people. They intentionally and methodically hurt others. Their behavior and thinking patterns don't just ruin the lives of those abused now, but affect generations. Their thinking and reasoning are broken. They think differently from others and that creates a dangerous and unpredictable individual.

Take all reasonable explanations about behavior and throw them out. When your thinking is warped you will not reason that your behavior is abusive or abnormal. Because of these broken thought processes, abusers believe they are entitled, yes, *entitled* to exploit others and will exploit others as long as they are permitted. They believe they are superior to their partners and therefore justified in their abuse. Patterns of blame will always be their partners' fault. Problems at work?

Struggling with coworkers or friends? Poor parenting? Addiction? All of these problems have a common cause, their partner. Couples in an abusive relationship are not equals. Abusers believe they own their partner and, since the partner is perceived as an object instead of a person, abusers think they have the right to treat them as they see fit. They derive their pleasure through dominance, not pain. They do not believe they are in the wrong, and as such, are unwilling (not unable) to relinquish their power and control in relationships. Only they benefit from their actions. Only they can stop the abuse. They are not out of control. They are making a choice.[86]

Victim: One night we had some friends over. My heart sank as they were leaving; I dreaded being alone with him. I remember so distinctly him standing at the door pleasantly waving goodbye and thanking everybody for coming. As soon as he closed the door, his head swiveled toward me like a scene in The Exorcist. *"Who the f*** do you think you are? You think you're so..." The berating and accusing went on and on and on as he spewed his perceptions of my faults. I just remember he was so calm and controlled one minute to our guests and so totally enraged at me the next.*

Abusers are experts at manipulating and twisting situations to justify their abuse. They falsely profess love. We all need to understand and acknowledge that abuse is the opposite of love. Abusers can be extremely concerned about their image in public, frequently presenting themselves as generous and charming, although their families will tell a different story.

"Researchers tell us that boys who grow up in homes where their mother is battered are more likely than other boys to grow up to abuse their own wives and girlfriends...At the same time, many men who abuse women–roughly one-half, in fact–did not learn their values and behaviors from their fathers or step-fathers, but instead absorbed abusive attitudes from peers, other male relatives, television, or from pornography."[87]

According to Lundy (2002), abusers may fit one of these types, a variation of these types, or none of these types:

- The man who demands his needs be met because it is his right. He is **entitled** to have his world revolve around him. His needs always take priority over the needs of others. He has a skewed perception of his contributions to the relationship. He believes his partner should be grateful to have such a wonderful partner as he.

- The man who **knows everything** about everything. He dismisses or discredits her thoughts and ideas, often with ridicule. He pretends to enjoy debates but is only interested in imposing his beliefs on others.

- The man who calmly, cruelly, and deliberately **provokes** her to an outburst. He easily convinces others she is the one with the problem.

- The man who **controls** her every move. He must run every detail of her life. He controls all of her relationships. He invades her privacy by monitoring her phone calls, checking her electronic devices, and asking others to monitor her activities. He frequently accuses her of being unfaithful while he is the one out running around. He is extremely jealous.

- The man who has studied self-help extensively. He uses what he has learned against his partner to **attack her vulnerabilities** and offers platitudes when she reacts negatively. He throws around all the right terms to make others believe he can't possibly be abusive. Nothing is more important than how he feels.

- The man who **sees women as playthings** and his to exploit sexually. It's not his fault he is so desirable. He enjoys the benefits of having more than one woman in his life at a time. He enjoys pitting the women against one another, diverting attention away from his roaming ways and lies. He carelessly disregards their feelings and may become physical when his actions are challenged, or he is caught cheating.

- The man who **enjoys creating fear** in everyone through intimidation. He has little patience for any sign of weakness. He is a protector of his trophy woman until she needs protecting from him. She is here to serve him. He has to keep her in line.

- The man who claims he has been a **victim** all his life: his family, his teachers, his boss, his ex all treated him wrongly. It's okay to hurt others because he's been hurt. He's had a "rough life" so all should excuse his actions.

- The man who constantly reminds his partner how her life is in his hands. He **terrorizes her** with statements of how he can/will hurt her. He perversely enjoys terrifying her with talk of cruelty. He paralyzes her with fear of ever leaving, often using threats of hurting the children.[88]

"An abuser is any person who has chronic, reoccurring problems with disrespecting, controlling, insulting, or devaluing his partner which seriously impacts the life of another, often leading to feelings of confusion, depression, anxiety, and fear."[89]

The core problem with abusive men is how they think. They adamantly defend and excuse their abusive behavior, even when expressing guilt about it. They almost never do anything that they believe crosses a moral line. The problem is they have a distorted sense of what is right and wrong. They are reluctant to face the devastation their abuse has caused their families. They believe they are justified in controlling and abusing their partner.[90]

The more comfortable he is with his behavior, the less remorse he will feel, and the more justifications for that behavior will increase. He has no problem denying the abuse happened or minimizing it as though it were no big deal.

Victim: One night, he came home after being out late and bit me for no apparent reason. The bruise was several inches in size and quite noticeable the next day. When I showed him the bruise, hoping for some kind of an explanation, his response was a flippant, "Oh. Sorry," and he went back to what he was doing. There was no further conversation about it. The bruise lasted for days.

His excuses for abuse are many. He was abused as a child so she thinks he needs counseling. (Counseling doesn't work to change abusive behavior.) Previous bad relationships with women made him like this. (He is shifting the blame for abuse to past women in his life.) His "deep feelings of love" drive him to his actions. (Feelings don't determine abuse; attitudes and patterns of behavior do.) He explodes because his emotions just build up. (It's not about his emotions but his pattern of thinking.) He's just an aggressive guy. (Most abusers are calm and reasonable in public and only become abusive in private.) He just loses control and goes berserk. (He gives himself permission to let go and do whatever he feels like doing.) He is also the victim of the relationship. (He isn't the one traumatized by years of assault.) Social oppression as a man of color is responsible for his need for power at home. (Men socially oppressed often are the most vocal in the fight against domestic violence.)

Her excuses for his abuse can also be many. He needs anger-management training. (His anger doesn't make him abusive; he is angry *because* he is abusive.) He is mentally ill and needs medication. (No known medication has been effective in turning an abuser into a kind, loving, supportive partner.) He has good reason to hate women. (He feels superior or contemptuous toward women, not hate.) He just has low self-esteem. (In reality, he expects to be catered to and told how wonderful he is.) His boss/job is responsible for how he behaves. (Research shows an improved job situation did little or nothing to stop the abuse at home.) He is poor at resolving conflicts, managing stress, and overall communication. (He does fine in situations with others; he is unwilling, not unable, to use proper skills when it in-

volves his partner.) If he stops drinking, everything will be okay. (Alcohol
doesn't create an abuser nor does so-
briety cure one.)[91]

> ALCOHOL DOESN'T
> CREATE AN ABUSER
> NOR DOES SOBRIETY
> CURE ONE.

Domestic violence recurrence ranks
among the highest in violent crimes.[92]
Prosecution of offenders is often more
difficult because of the ongoing emotional relationship between the
abuser and the victim. Abusers often present as charming, persuasive
and logical, even to trained personnel.

*Victim: Another victim wanted to file a report against her abuser
for violating his order to stay away from her. He had left some of her
personal items outside her home while she was away, so she reported a
violation of the protection order. The prosecutor did not see there was a
violation once she questioned the abuser because he claimed he was just
trying to be nice and give her back stuff he knew she'd want. He hadn't
bothered her; he'd made a point to go when she wasn't home. As victims,
we view it differently than the prosecutor. We know how he thinks. We
know he was sending the victim a message: I can get to you anytime,
anywhere and get away with it. He was letting her know a piece of paper
wasn't going to stop him. He was letting her know he could and would do
whatever. Out of curiosity, eleven other victims were asked their opinion
of the case. All eleven polled agreed with the victim– he was sending her
a message.*

Spiritual Truths about Abusers

The Bible is clear on the truth about abuse in any form. Any excuse
for mistreating a partner is distorted thinking. There are not only psychological and behavioral characteristics of abusers, but also spiritual
characteristics. We know that we are all sinners and have fallen short
of the glory of God (Romans 3:23), but those of us who have been
saved by grace have been changed.

While the abuser is a sinner, the difference is, he has an evil heart and no wish to change. Proverbs 6:12-14 (ESV) reads, *"A worthless person, a wicked man, goes about with crooked speech, winks with his eyes, signals with his feet, points with his finger, with perverted heart devises evil, continually sowing discord."* We know that Scripture shows us that God hates all evil. He doesn't miss a single infraction committed against His children. Psalm 11:5 (ESV) says, *"The Lord tests the righteous, but His soul hates the wicked and the one who loves violence."* No one knows our hearts more than our Heavenly Father. If we are filled with love, we will speak and act abundantly from love. If our heart is filled with evil, our actions, words, and behaviors will reveal evil. *"For as he thinks in his heart, so is he"* (Proverbs 23:7a NLT).

Within that selfish and evil heart is a need for abusers to have their own way. They are inherently selfish and will make sure to get their way, by whatever means necessary. No amount of trampled bodies will get in the way. *"Then the Lord saw that the wickedness of man was great in the earth, and that every intent of the thoughts of his heart was only evil continually"*(Genesis 6:5 NKJV).

An abuser is not only a breaker of man's laws but a breaker of God's laws. He disobeys Christ. John Piper in his article, "Clarifying Words on Wife Abuse" makes this very point:

> Every Christian is called to submit to various authorities and to each other: children to parents (Ephesians 6:1), citizens to government (Romans 13:1), wives to husbands (Ephesians 5:22), employees to employers (2 Thessalonians 3:10), church members to elders (Hebrews 13:17), all Christians to each other (Ephesians 5:21), all believers to Christ (Luke 6:46).

> This puts the submission of wives and husbands into the wider context of submission to Jesus, to the civil authorities, to each other, and to the church. This means that the rightness or wrongness of any act of submission is discerned by taking into account all the relevant relationships. We are all responsible to Jesus first, and then, under Him, to various other persons and

offices. Discerning the path of love and obedience when two or more of these submissive relationships collide is a call to humble, Bible-saturated, spiritual wisdom.

Husbands are commanded, "Love your wives, and do not be harsh with them" (Colossians 3:19). They are told to "love their wives as their own bodies. He who loves his wife loves himself. For no one ever hated his own flesh, but nourishes and cherishes it" (Ephesians 5:28-29). The focus of a husband's Christlikeness in loving his wife is "love your wives, as Christ loved the church and *gave himself up for her*" (Ephesians 5:25).

Therefore, an abusive husband is breaking God's law. He is disobeying Christ. He is not to be indulged but disciplined by the church. The wife is not insubordinate to ask the church for help. A Christian woman should not feel that the only help available to her is the police. That would be a biblical failure of her church.[93]

An abuser is deceived. He does not believe God loves him. He has not been taught how to love. He believes love is conditional. Scripture tells us, *"He who does not love does not know God, for God is love"* (1 John 4:8 NKJV). Abusers struggle to authentically share love because they truly don't know or understand love. They are ruled by their fears, and they use that same fear to rule others. *"There is no fear in love. But perfect love drives out fear, because fear has to do with punishment. The one who fears is not made of perfect love"*(1 John 4:18 NIV).

Abusive behavior comes from a person's heart, their experiences, and their environment. He may even have experienced abuse himself. Regardless of how we were raised or the experiences we have had, there is always the choice to perpetuate violence or love. Proverbs 22:6 (ESV) becomes even more important than we might first realize. *"Train up a child in the way he should go, and when he is old he will not depart from it."*

Common Characteristics of Abusers

There is no way to pick an abuser out of a crowd. There is no social class, education level, religious/political beliefs, race, or economic status that determines an abuser. Most abusers are male, although most males do not abuse. Men choose abuse to achieve compliance and control of their partner.

"Men batter because it works. Domestic violence is a socially supported behavior learned through observation, experience, and reinforcement. It is learned through our culture, families, schools, and peer groups. Domestic violence is not caused by illness, genetics, substance abuse, stress, the behavior of the victim, or problems in the relationship".[94]

Victim: I had an opportunity to speak to a group of men in a batters program. After sharing pieces of my story, we had a time of questions and answers. One man asked me, "You said he did all that? What did you do?" At first, I thought he was blaming me. Then he clarified he was asking about my response to the abuse. I answered, "I didn't do anything. I was too scared! He was bigger than me and stronger than me. If I couldn't escape, I just tried to be invisible and hope he wouldn't notice me. I had a child to protect." The man leaned back in his chair and crossed his arms before responding. "You didn't do anything? Well, that's the problem. That man didn't have any consequences. He's not going to stop. Why should he? Nothing happens to him when he does that." His answer was like a punch in the stomach taking my breath. After a moment of silence, I had to ask my burning question, "What should I have done?" He leaned forward, "Left. You should have left. You don't need to put up with that stuff." Other men in the group nodded in agreement. This advice from the very men who are abusers. Their honesty seared my soul.

Abusers that also have children will have a common tool they can use to further manipulate. There are many ways this can be done. An abuser can punish the children verbally, physically, and/or sexually to hurt the victim. They can make the children watch their parent be abused, or even force them to participate in the abuse. Children are often used to spy on their parent and report back. Other tactics can include threatening to kidnap, harm or kill the children if she leaves. In cases of custodial struggles, abusers can use custody or visitation arrangements to harm/harass her, and in severe cases, gain legal custody just to take the children to harass/harm her.

Victim: Our marriage was one big double standard. I was forbidden to talk to certain family members of his because they were doing drugs–yet he was doing drugs. I got reamed if he called and I didn't answer the first time, yet he wouldn't even answer his phone when I called. I had to make my plans way in advance and let him know about them, but he could change plans or create new ones on the spur of the moment and not even tell me. He would spend literally hundreds of dollars in the bar, but I got humiliated for giving too much to the church. I could never disagree with what he said or did, but he had no problem telling me how stupid and wrong I was. Even when he accused me, saying, "Who are you f***ing now?" I found out later he was the one cheating.

In a healthy relationship, equality is experienced by both parties. In a domestic violence relationship, the inequality of power is not present/obvious at the beginning. It is over time that the abuser becomes more and more demanding that his needs be met. He uses power and control to get what he wants. (See Resources 3 and 4)

HE USES POWER AND CONTROL TO GET WHAT HE WANTS.

For though we walk in the flesh, we do not war according to the flesh. For the weapons of our warfare are not carnal but mighty in God for pulling down strongholds, casting down arguments and every high thing that exalts itself against the knowledge of God, bringing every thought into captivity to the obedience of Christ, and being ready to punish all disobedience when your obedience is fulfilled.
2 Corinthians 10:3-6 NKJV

Chapter 9

Why Doesn't She Just Leave?

Do not become partners with those who do not believe, for what partnership is there between righteousness and lawlessness, or what fellowship does light have with darkness? 2 Corinthians 6:14 NET

The first question that women who are trapped in domestic violence are often asked is, "Why don't you just leave?" From the outside looking in, it can seem an easy answer. If someone is hurting you, why would you stay? The hard truth is that many abused women, especially women of faith, do not see themselves as being abused. They are reluctant to leave their husband, as they have a high regard for an intact family. These women are especially prone to blame themselves for the abuse.

These women take their marriage vow to love and honor their husbands till death as a promise to be kept. They feel a responsibility to keep forgiving and remain ever hopeful that their abuser will change. They are reluctant to reach out to secular, community-based resources for support, preferring to seek help from like-minded clergy and lay persons. Should they end the relationship, they feel shame, and they fear rejection from others in their church.[95]

"For I hate divorce," says the Lord, the God of Israel, "and him who covers his garment with wrong and violence," says the Lord of hosts. "Therefore keep watch on your spirit, so that you do not deal treacherously [with your wife]." Malachi 2:16 AMP

The Cycle of Violence

Like many things in life, domestic violence often follows a cyclical pattern. The cycle of violence theory was developed in 1979 by psychologist Dr. Lenore Walker who found many violent relationships follow a common pattern.[96] It is generally composed of three major parts: the tension-building phase, the explosive phase, and the calm/loving phase (sometimes called the honeymoon phase).

We know that over the course of most abuse, the amount of time to complete each cycle lessens and the explosions escalate in severity. When considering how to best minister to victims, it is important to understand this cycle so that you can help her understand the dynamics of intimate partner abuse.

"The cycle of violence looks at the repetitive nature of the perpetrator's actions that hinder a victim's ability to leave an abusive relationship. The cycle of violence theory provides an insight into this by illustrating how the behavior of a perpetrator can change very dramatically, making it difficult for the woman to leave. Women who have experienced violence may recognize this cycle."[97]

A simple representation is shown below.

In the first phase, women often describe the feeling of walking on egg shells. Slamming doors, throwing objects, and yelling generally occur. She senses it is just a matter of time before the abuser escalates. A heightened sensitivity begins as she becomes very alert to his words, actions, body language, and reactions. This creates stress and tension as she hopes to respond in ways that prevent or delay the abuse. She will try to make sure nothing she or the children do provokes him. She may become quiet, withdrawn, more passive, more submissive, and

CYCLE OF VIOLENCE

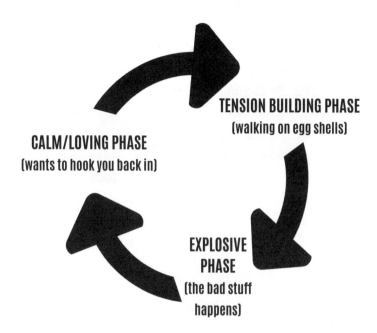

TENSION BUILDING PHASE
(walking on egg shells)

CALM/LOVING PHASE
(wants to hook you back in)

EXPLOSIVE PHASE
(the bad stuff happens)

more agreeable. She will try harder to please him. She may try to avoid him and her children may be warned to be quiet and stay out of sight. She may try to keep family and friends away. She may try to reason with or calm her abuser.

In contrast, the abuser is moody, harsh, overly critical, and sensitive. He may begin yelling at her and calling her names. He may try and provoke her to argue. He may embarrass her in front of family or friends. He may accuse her of unfaithfulness. He may threaten her or the children. He may isolate her from others. He may destroy property. He may withhold attention or affection. He may engage in alcohol or drug use. Sadly, everything she says or does is futile. We know that regardless what she tries, the explosion will come. *There is no smoothing things over.* Although the abuse may be blamed on her or the children, the abuse is not caused by her or her children's actions. The abuser will find an excuse to abuse because he is an abuser. It is a deliberate choice on his part designed to exert power and control over his intimate partner.[98]

Victim: I could always sense when he would explode soon. The tension in the air was palpable. The slamming and banging would start. The threats and hurtful comments would come next. As hard as I tried to please him, I knew the explosion was coming. Nothing could stop it, only fleetingly delay it. By watching his every move and listening to every nuance in his voice, I became better at gauging when to try and escape.

The second phase is where the explosive behavior happens. He exhibits extreme, unpredictable actions she cannot stop or control. Even if the explosion starts as verbal/emotional abuse, the chances of the abuse becoming physical are great. She knows there is little chance of escape. She is terrified, often paralyzed with fear. He may choke her, punch her, kick her, degrade her, humiliate her, cut her, burn her, imprison her, rape her, or more. At this point, the victim is simply trying to survive the attack and protect herself in whatever way she thinks will help her do so. The abuse can continue for minutes or days. She may or may not fight back. In this phase, the police may be called. She may be in shock and not report the incident for days or at all. Child protective services agencies may be involved. She may escape to safety. She may seek protection from him. She may refuse to talk to him or see him. At this point, the woman is most likely to leave the relationship. She may begin to experience sadness, anger, and helplessness.[99]

Victim: I get asked if I ever fought back. No, I didn't. The truth was I was too scared. I always just tried to escape if I could. I have no doubt that had I fought back, the abuse would have escalated quickly, and I would have sustained massive injuries. When I couldn't leave, I believe God gave me the grace just to stand there and let his words spew all over me. Whatever he demanded, I did. I tried not to react as he stood over me as I waited fearfully to see how far he would take his abuse this time. I could feel my eyes glazing over and myself detaching as I waited for what was coming. He asked me once why I never fought back. Was I that good at hiding my fear? He was so much bigger and stronger that I wouldn't stand a chance. Within a few years of our relationship ending, he was arrested for severely beating another woman and was sentenced to prison for several years. But for the grace of God, that could have been me.

In the final stage, the abuser realizes he has lost his power and control over his victim, so the abuser will now try a variety of tactics to get his partner to return. This phase is where his calm, loving side shows up. Some refer to this as the honeymoon phase. He may start feeling ashamed and exhibit some remorse. He may apologize and promise it will never happen again. He may try to justify his behavior to her and others. He may try and woo her with flowers or gifts. He lets her know she is the only one he loves and other women aren't important. He may say he can't live without her; he will die without her. He may promise to stop drinking or doing drugs. He may promise to go to church or counseling. He may go to anger management classes. He may promise to get a job or support her in getting one. He may get family and friends to feel sorry for him and pressure her to return. He may tell her she is the only one who truly understands him, the only one who can help him. He may promise to be a better partner and parent. He insists he has already changed. The promises go on and on. He tells her everything he believes will make her return to him so he can reestablish his power and control over her. She may be flattered with all this romantic behavior. She longs for that closeness they first shared. With such a barrage of seemingly sincere, loving words the victim has wanted to hear, with hope that this time he means it, with the belief that this time will be different, she may choose to return to her abuser. Intimacy can increase in this phase. Both may minimize the severity of the abuse and refuse to admit the possibility of the violence recurring. She may experience a time of peace and happiness as he shows her kindness as he did in the beginning of the relationship, but it is only a matter of time before the abuse begins anew. Had she understood the cycle of violence, she might have seen through his insincerity and manipulation.[100]

Although it is not shown on the diagram, if the last phase where he is calm and loving doesn't work in getting her to reestablish the relationship, the abuser may again resort to direct threats to harm her, her loved ones, or himself. Threats of suicide are not uncommon. He may destroy her property. He may spread rumors about her to ruin her reputation. He may reveal information told to him in confidence to humiliate her. He may pursue her relentlessly. He may flip back and forth between being charming and threatening, desperately searching for the tactic that will get her to return this time. His full focus is on regaining his control over her. Her fear of his threats may push all logical reasoning out of her mind. She may be convinced he will never leave her alone so she may as well go back. Even knowing the cycle of violence may not stop her from returning to him. She is again under his power and control.[101]

Victim: He threatened "If you don't come back, I'll take our daughter and you'll never see her again. You think you can find her, but I know people all over the country. You'll never find her. Nobody will tell you where she is. How does that work for you?" I went back.

Understanding the cycle of violence better prepares the victim for her abuser's tactics. Her support system can help her. She can look for his manipulation whether in the form of flattery and promises or threats and intimidation. She is then able to make a more informed choice about remaining separate or returning to the relationship.

From what we know about the cycle of violence, once she returns to the abusive relationship, the cycle will start all over again. It may take days or even weeks before his promises are broken, and she finds herself right back in the same situation. Why should he stop doing what he is doing when what he is doing gets him what he wants? A *very low* percentage of abusers stop abusing.[102] Even then, effective intervention and a sincere desire to change must occur. Abuse is a learned behavior. It is a choice. The responsibility for abuse lies fully with the abuser.[103]

For the cycle of abuse to be broken, one person in the relationship must change. Either the abuser must stop abusing or the abused must stop accepting abuse. The abusive man needs to stop perceiving his mate as a piece of property and instead recognize that he is inflicting pain on a precious person created in the image of God – a person highly valued by God. This change of mind-set will make a real difference. The abused woman needs to place her dependence on God rather than falsely believing she cannot function without her abusive man. A change in mind-set will change an abusive relationship.[104]

Victim: I left so many times– sometimes for hours or days, sometimes for weeks and months. I filed for divorce a total of three times. I filed for orders of protection more than once. I even moved out and got an apartment for several months. Every time, I believed him when he said he would do whatever it took for us to be a family again. I wanted to believe it would be different this time. Each time I went back, for a while, things were like they were before, when he was his charming best. The make-up sex was great. We went to church together. We did attend a few counseling sessions. He did take medication for a while. He did stop drinking and doing drugs. He wasn't out running around. But after a while, all the promises were broken. The roller coaster started again. Mr. Prince Charming with your lips full of lies...

I WANTED TO BELIEVE IT WOULD BE DIFFERENT THIS TIME.

Barriers to Leaving

Those outside the abusive relationship may think leaving should be simple: pack up your things and go. Each woman has her own complex, individual reasons she stays with, goes back to, or truly leaves her abuser. Just as abuse is progressive, leaving an abusive situation is progressive. Leaving is fraught with fear and uncertainty. Instilling fear is a powerful weapon when used to control another person. The average victim may leave her abuser many times before leaving for the final time. Each time she goes back reinforces his power and control over her.

Victim: When I was told abused women leave their abuser an average of seven times, I figured a lot of women got to leave a whole lot sooner than me. I had left so many more than seven times. Every time, I thought it would be different; every time, it wasn't. I wonder how different my life would have been had I just stayed gone the first time.

The Power of Coercion

Rebecca Bender compiled a list of tactics abusers admit using to maintain power and control over their victims.[105] These tactics, slightly modified for our purposes, are shared in the following four paragraphs.

I would **isolate** her, breaking her ties with any support she had. I'd convince her family and friends that I was the good one. I took all of the money and made it inaccessable so that she depended on me for everything. If she was leaving to visit with friends and family, I would start a fight right before so that eventually, she just stopped visiting. I moved her way out in the country or to another city. When I left, I took her car battery with me. I convinced the people around her that she was crazy, imagined things, and needed counseling. I could prove it by pointing out her erratic behavior. That way, she had nowhere to go if she tried to leave. I convinced everyone around her that she was incapable of caring for the children because of her stupidity, mental illness, and laziness. I ripped the phone cord out of the wall during a fight when she tried to call for help or threw her cell phone. I had her back me up on illegal things so that I could hold it over her head if she tried to leave.

I'd use **gaslighting** to make her doubt her sanity and capabilities. I'd convince her she was crazy by playing mind games with her. I'd hide her things and tell her how incompetent she was so that she'd believe me when I told her that she needed me. I kept her up in the night so she was easier to control the next day. I turned the kids against her by making her the bad parent and tricking the children. I would make her hit the children by saying, "Either you hit them, or I will," (knowing I hit harder), and then threaten to report her for child abuse if she left me. I made her feel guilty about wanting to break up our family, that she was being a bad mother and wife if she wanted to leave every time things got difficult. I told her how fat and ugly she was all the time, and how badly she did things around the house. I told her how embarrassed I was of her. I told her that no one else would want my sloppy seconds, that she was used goods. I'd rape her. Anything to make her feel unworthy of respect, love, and care.

I **made her afraid** of leaving me. I told her that women's shelters were for women who really needed it, not for women who wanted to give up on their family. I made sure she knew that she wouldn't get a dime from me if she left and that she'd be poor and homeless. I ruined her credit by putting things in her name and not paying for them. I followed her without her knowing so that I could make her believe I had people watching her. I threatened suicide. I told her I would kill her and I threatened to hurt people she loved. I would lock up all of her things, including the social security cards, birth certificates, and pictures. I broke things and told her that it was her fault for upsetting me. I reminded her of the last time she left me, that it only made things worse. I told her that I'd never let her go, no matter what it took. I convinced her that I'd find her wherever she went. I always kept one of the kids with me, so I knew that she'd always come back.

I **convinced her that I deserved another chance**. That I was sorry for what I'd done. I cried to her. I made countless empty promises. Promised to change my ways. I promised to go to drug and alcohol treatment and counseling. I blamed the abuse on stress. I romanced her with flowers, took her shopping, talking about all the good times, and telling her how much she meant to me. I even arranged for us to take a romantic trip together to get back on track. I made her think she needed to stick by me because of all I gave up to be with her. I made her feel sorry for me, and that her love could change me.

Leaving a violent relationship is not a simple matter. As hard as it is for friends and family to understand, sometimes she is just not ready to walk away for good. She hasn't reached the place where there is nothing he can say or do to get her to stay or return. Remember, abusers are masters at manipulation. He not only manipulates his partner, but law enforcement, the court system, counselors, clergy, and even close family and friends.[106] It is important to empower the victim and allow her to determine when is the best time for her to leave.[107] There may need to be a period of preparation, often called "Safety Planning." (See Resources 5 and 6) There are many factors that must be weighed carefully.

Barriers to leaving may include:

- Loving the part of him that isn't abusive and she is the only one who knows how to love him

- Believing abuse is normal or deserved and denial of the danger she is in

- Pride won't let her admit her marriage is a failure or depend on others

- Believing he loves her more than anyone ever has and false hope in promises he will change

- Assessing it is safer to stay as he may become more violent or deadly if she leaves

- Fear of escalation of violence/abuse tactics by the abuser and fear of the unknown

- Abuser having powerful job or social/business connections

- Being sick, disabled, or elderly

- Fear of losing custody/visitation of the children to the abuser and false allegations of child abuse/neglect by the abuser

- Fear of him reporting her illegal (forced) activity

- Lack of income/lack of finances, of housing, transportation and childcare

- Bowing to family/friend pressure, no support system

- Viewing him as a father figure

- Loneliness or isolation, damage of possessions

- Misguided secular/clerical counselors focusing on saving the relationship, not stopping abuse

- Believing her value as a woman depends on getting and keeping a man

- Believing she is pleasing God by staying and a desperation to keep her family intact

- Fear of threats and retaliation being carried out

- Misplaced sense of gratitude, addiction to the adrenaline high when times are good

- Believing her success or failure in marriage is her responsibility and equals her failure as a person; unwarranted/false guilt or shame

- Rationalizing that the abuse is caused by outside influences (job loss, stress, alcohol, etc.)

- Religious or cultural beliefs may not support divorce or may support male dominance

- Lack of education/skills, unaware of help and available options

- Past criminal record, substance or alcohol abuse

- Being an undocumented illegal immigrant

- Failure of courts to hold abusers accountable for violations of protection orders or to prosecute and sentence effectively

- Minimized abuse by law enforcement and first responders; lack of training for law enforcement regarding domestic violence where victims are arrested

The time in which a victim leaves the situation and the abuser realizes he is losing power and control is the most dangerous time for her and others. "Domestic violence does not always end when the victim escapes the abuser, tries to terminate the relationship, and/or seeks help. Often, it intensifies because the abuser feels a loss of control over the victim. Abusers frequently continue to stalk, harass, threaten, and try to control the victim after the victim escapes. In fact, the victim is often in the most danger directly following the escape of the relationship or when they seek help: 1/5 of homicide victims with restraining orders are murdered within two days of obtaining the order; 1/3 are murdered within the first month."[108]

It may be safer for her to stay because the abuser threatens more violence if she leaves. He may threaten to kill her, her children, and/or her family/friends. Her experience with his past violence/abuse shows he will follow through with threats. "Twenty percent of the homicides [at the time of leaving] were not the domestic violence victim herself but family, friends, neighbors, law enforcement, people who tried to help, or bystanders."[109] With children involved, there is always a real fear that he will gain custody or that he will get unsupervised visits with the children during which she is unable to monitor his interactions with them. (See Resource 7)

THE TIME IN WHICH A VICTIM LEAVES THE SITUATION AND THE ABUSER REALIZES HE IS LOSING POWER AND CONTROL IS THE MOST DANGEROUS TIME FOR HER AND OTHERS.

Possible Risks to the Victim When Leaving the Relationship

Many times, there is not a lot of difference in the amount of abuse that occurs while in the relationship and after leaving. Below is a list of behaviors comparing what can happen to a victim if she stays compared to what can happen to a victim if she leaves.[110]

- If she stays ➜ he can continue to harm her.
  If she leaves ➜ he might continue to harm her. The violence might escalate.

- If she stays ➜ he may kill her or the children.
  If she leaves ➜ it might increase the chance that she or the children will be killed. Leaving doesn't insure he won't find her.

- If she stays➜ children can witness the violence, be targets, or become hurt trying to protect others.
  If she leaves ➜ children can witness the violence, be targets, or become hurt trying to protect others. They might be at greater risk during visitations.

- If she stays ➜ he could make false allegations of her abuse/neglect of the children. Failure-to-protect arguments can be used to remove the children from the home or terminate parental rights.
  If she leaves ➜ he could make false allegations of child abuse or neglect. He could legally gain custody of the children or just take them.

- If she stays ➜ she might have no choice regarding safe sex practices. He might sexually assault her.
  If she leaves ➜ unsafe sexual behavior may continue. He might sexually assault her.

- If she stays ➜ he could keep her from working or limit how much she works. He might sabotage her job hunt, her job success, or her completion of school or training.
  If she leaves ➜ she might have to quit her job or leave school. He might sabotage her efforts to find or keep a job or succeed in school or training.

- If she stays ➜ he might destroy things of importance or value to her.
  If she leaves ➜ he might destroy things of importance or value to her. She might have to leave valued items behind.

- If she stays ➜ she might be evicted because of property damage he has done.
  If she leaves ➜ she might have to move out, leave town, or go into hiding. She might lose her home in a divorce.

- If she stays ➜ he might threaten or injure family/friends, particularly if they try to help.
  If she leaves ➜ he might threaten or injure family/friends, particularly if they try to help.

- If she stays ➜ family/friends might want her to leave and remove support if she stays.
  If she leaves ➜ family/friends may not agree that she should leave. They might stop supporting her.

- If she stays ➜ he might control the money and give her little on which to live. He could lose/quit his job or make her quit hers.
  If she leaves ➜ she might have to live on even less money. She might have to move out of her home and community.

- If she stays ➜ abusive attacks will continue to affect her.
  If she leaves ➜ abusive attacks may continue, particularly if they share children.

- If she stays ➜ she might use drugs or alcohol to help her cope with the emotional and physical pain.
  If she leaves ➜ she might use drugs or alcohol to help her cope with her new situation and past abuse.

- If she stays ➜ he might threaten or commit suicide.
  If she leaves ➜ he might threaten or commit suicide.

- If she stays ➜ he might undermine or interfere with her parenting.
  If she leaves ➜ he might undermine or interfere with her parenting.

My heart falters, fear makes me tremble… Isaiah 21:4 NIV

It's incredibly difficult to comprehend the fear that these daughters of God are living with daily and the obstacles that they face when they finally seek solace and freedom outside of abuse. As survivors, they may feel overwhelmed by the sheer number of resources available to help them, but we can make sure that those resources are easier to access. We can build a space of trust where these women can reach out, be honest, be heard, and know there is help for them and their children. On average, nearly 20 people per minute are physically abused by an intimate partner in the United States. The Church has a responsibility to stand with these victims and proclaim, "You are not alone," and to inform abusers, "This sin against God's children will not be tolerated." **Rather than asking the victim why she doesn't just leave the abuse, we should be asking the abuser why he doesn't just stop the abuse.**

ON AVERAGE, NEARLY 20 PEOPLE PER MINUTE ARE PHYSICALLY ABUSED BY AN INTIMATE PARTNER IN THE UNITED STATES.

Chapter 10

Why Does She Finally Leave?

He reveals the deep things of darkness and brings
utter darkness into the light. Job 12:22 NIV

Leaving something you expected to last forever is one of the hardest things to do. Leaving because your partner, who was charged to love, honor, and care for you is making you fearful for your life, the lives of your children, and even the lives of those you love, creates an emotional blockade that must be overcome if freedom is to be achieved. Leaving an abusive relationship is a process requiring the victim to go through several changes in beliefs:

- She must recognize her relationship is dangerous.

- She must realize the relationship will not get better.

- She must experience an event that serves as a catalyst to leaving.

- She must give up her dream of what she expected from the relationship.

- She must accept that, to some extent, the relationship will never be over if there are children involved.[111]

Victim: As a Christian woman, I agonized for years over wanting to leave my husband. At first, I really didn't want to leave; I just wanted the abuse to stop. As the years passed, I felt guilty as my love for him gradually died with each instance of abuse. I spent hours on my face before God trying to figure out what to do. I talked to pastors and counselors who had no idea the advice they gave was so wrong for my situation. I never told them I was abused because I didn't know I was abused. I was so torn– I wanted to leave, but I didn't want to break my vows. I knew God as a loving God who couldn't possibly be okay with the abuse, yet I was aware of the Scriptures related to marriage. I didn't know what I know now. I didn't know that while God hates divorce, He also hates violence. The straw that broke the camel's back for me was finding out he was sleeping with another woman– again. It may be hard to understand, but I was actually relieved when I discovered my husband's infidelity. I had already forgiven him for being unfaithful a few years prior. I could now end the marriage with less guilt: God said it was okay to leave in cases of adultery. My decision to divorce was based more on his infidelity than his alcohol and drug use and my years of abuse. For so long, I held on to the hope he was going to change, and we would have such a glorious testimony. It didn't happen, and I finally admitted it wasn't going to happen. He had no interest in changing. The other woman was "just a friend." He was only a "recreational" drug user. He "liked his beer." I wonder how much longer I might have stayed had I not discovered he was cheating.

> IF MARRIAGE ENDANGERS THE PHYSICAL, EMOTIONAL, OR SPIRITUAL WELL-BEING OF OTHERS, SERIOUS CONSIDERATION MUST BE GIVEN AS TO THE CONSEQUENCES OF REMAINING MARRIED.

In the faith community, marriage is a matter of utmost importance, especially if children are involved. Ending it is not to be considered lightly. However, if marriage endangers the physical, emotional, or spiritual well-being of others, serious consideration must be given as to the consequences of remaining married.

It may be helpful to point out to Christian victims the Scriptures relating well-known figures leaving a violent situation. The Bible gives examples of Moses, David, Joseph, Jesus, and Paul leaving when facing harm:

When Pharaoh heard of it, he sought to kill Moses.
But Moses fled from Pharaoh and stayed in the land of Midian.
And he sat down by a well. Exodus 2:15 ESV

And Saul sought to pin David to the wall with the spear, but he
eluded Saul, so that he struck the spear into the wall. And David
fled and escaped that night. Saul sent messengers to David's house
to watch him, that he might kill him in the morning. But Michal,
David's wife, told him, "If you do not escape with your life tonight,
tomorrow you will be killed." So Michal let David down through the
window, and he fled away and escaped. 1 Samuel 19:10-12 ESV

Now when they had departed, behold, an angel of the Lord
appeared to Joseph in a dream, saying, "Arise, take the
young Child and His mother, flee to Egypt, and stay there
until I bring you word; for Herod will seek the young Child
to destroy Him." Matthew 2:13 NKJV

And they rose up and drove him [Jesus]out of the town and brought
him to the brow of the hill on which their town was built, so that they
could throw him down the cliff. But passing through their midst, he
went away. Luke 4:29-30 ESV

At Damascus, the governor under King Aretas was guarding
the city of Damascus in order to seize me, [Paul] but I was let down

> ### *in a basket through a window in the wall and escaped his hands.*
> ### *2 Corinthians 11:32-33 ESV*

While all of us earnestly desire that marriages in trouble are healed, the option of leaving and divorce must not be withheld from victims. Dr. Billy Graham addressed the issue of troubled marriages when one partner is in sin: "I would be less than honest with you if I did not tell you of the possibility that your marriage may never be restored. While it is God's will that every marriage will endure, man's sin has poisoned many relationships. You should pray for your husband, but you should also move forward with your own life and with what God might do in and through you."[112]

Only the woman in the domestic violence situation can make the decision of what is best for her and her family regarding the safety and timing of leaving her abuser. "Often, survivors tell us, the bitterest parts of abuse happen after the marriage has ended. Of domestic murders, 75 percent occur before, during or after the victim has attempted to leave. As the couple separates, every sort of bitterness is unleashed."[113]

The victim's church family needs to be aware of the risks to her and her family when leaving and the turmoil that follows. They need to be aware that she will have a plethora of emotions and needs, immediately and over time. "Shaming and blaming do little to help, however much we may deplore the dissolution of a marriage. Most Christians already carry a tremendous sense of shame that their marriage has ended in divorce, and many cannot even face their old friends at church– just when they need them most."[114]

No matter how she feels now and what she says, she will likely return to her abuser several times before finally ending the relationship. The hope is always that the woman sees a path to permanently leave. Most women I know had either a "final straw" moment or an epiphany. In either case, it was the impetus she needed to leave and not return, regardless of his pleas, manipulations, promises, threats, or her own fears and emotions.

It is imperative that the woman is empowered to leave. Then decisions surrounding her leaving must be hers alone. As much as we might like to rescue her from her situation, we can't make decisions for her. It doesn't help her. As tempting as it is to want to rescue a victim, it doesn't keep her safe in the long run. Understandably, you desire to help. However, that desire is more a function of your need than hers.[115]

> You may care very deeply for an abused woman. You may want desperately to see that she doesn't get hurt or killed by her abusive partner. As hard as this may be for you to understand, by attempting to rescue her you are not *showing* your support of her. You are not *showing* her that you respect her or her abilities to make decisions and take actions to protect herself. *You are not helping her.* If you are rescuing her, you may actually be removing your support and disempowering her.

> To rescue a woman from her abusive partner or her life as it exists can even be an implied criticism of her. You are sending her a message that she could easily interpret as, "You are a screw up. You make bad decisions which have gotten you in this horrible mess. Since you are a bad decision maker and since I make better decisions than you, you should do what I am telling you, not what you are telling yourself!"[116]

The first critical step in leaving the relationship is for the victim to break away from being isolated. She must reach out to someone, somewhere. For Christians, the church could be that first contact that helps her understand she is not alone. The second critical step in leaving the relationship is for someone in her life to be supportive and encouraging. She must be convinced of her value.[117] She must understand she is not responsible for the abuse nor can she change it.[118]

Even to your old age and gray hairs I am he, I am he who will sustain you. I have made you and I will carry you; I will sustain you and I will rescue you. Isaiah 46:4 NIV

Below is a list of common reasons a victim will finally leave an abusive relationship.

- She finally leaves because she is afraid for the life of her children. She sees he has started to abuse the children or the abuse is increasing. She is unable to stop the abuse other than by leaving. Her older children may have started fighting back or intervening to protect her during the abuse, often escalating the violence.

- She finally leaves because she is afraid for her life. She realizes there is only a fine line between his threats to kill her and his actually killing her. She realizes she can't protect her children from him if she is dead.

- She finally leaves because she sees her children acting as violently as he does or using the same survival tactics that she does. She wants to prevent her children from adopting abusive mindsets and ways of behaving.

- She finally leaves because she has become educated in the dynamics of domestic violence. She recognizes the different types of abuse in her relationship. She can recognize which stage in the cycle of violence she is currently experiencing. She identifies his manipulative attempts to coerce and control.

- She finally leaves because she realizes he is not going to change as long as things remain the same. He must be willing to confess and sincerely repent of his sin of abuse, be held accountable for his actions, and take the proper steps to change his behavior. He must be motivated to change regardless of whether she remains in his life or not.

- She finally leaves because she has support through friends, family, church, and professional organizations. She realizes she is not alone.

- She finally leaves because she understands it is never God's will that anyone experience abuse. She is a person of value. Her abuser's lies about her do not line up with the word of God.

Let the evil of the wicked come to an end, but establish the righteous. The one who examines the thoughts and emotions is a righteous God.
Psalm 7:9 CSB

Women who leave need the aid of supportive family or friends in addition to the protective hand of God who guides and strengthens her. Again, her church family can and should be part of her support system. She needs everyone in her corner to help her realize her value as a beloved child of God.

Chapter 11

A Pastor's Response to Domestic Violence

Rescue me, O Lord, from evil men; preserve me from violent men
Who devise evil things in their hearts;
they continually stir up wars.
They sharpen their tongues as a serpent;
poison of a viper is under their lips. Selah.
Keep me, O Lord, from the hands of the wicked;
preserve me from violent men who have purposed
to trip up my feet. Psalm 140:1-4 NASB

Are you prepared? This may seem like an easy question, but joining someone inside of their painful reality can be tough.

Studies show that when a Christian woman seeks help in an abusive marriage, she ordinarily consults either her pastor or a woman in the congregation. The first lesson that we must teach pastors is that the danger is real and it takes a great courage for a woman to disclose the humiliating truth she's a victim. She is well aware that many a woman has been sent home by the pastor along with a rebuke that if she had been a better wife there would have been no problem. Thus she must struggle not only with the shame but also fear– fear that she will not be believed and fear that it may go worse for her at home once she has made a disclosure.[119]

In 2014, only 23% of 1,000 Protestant pastors surveyed who spoke to their churches about domestic or sexual violence reported having been trained in domestic violence issues. In 2018, the number doubled to 46%. However, despite increasing attention to this subject, 20% of pastors don't feel compelled to address domestic violence.[120] Most pastors admit little or no training in domestic violence, one-fifth seeing no need to address the issue. In North America, according to the Centers for Disease Control and Prevention, more than one-third to one-fourth of families experience abuse.[121] However, only 18% of Protestant pastors report domestic or sexual violence is a problem in their congregation.[122]

"Chuck Colson lamented: Tragically, studies reveal that spousal abuse is just as common within the evangelical churches as anywhere else. This means that about 25 percent of Christian homes witness abuse of some kind. In many Christian homes, domestic violence is a family value. How can any family be strong when one or more of its members live in fear of being hit, maimed, or killed in their own home by one of their own? Virtually no church, house of worship, or community is untouched by this act of sin."[123]

And yet, who better for believers who are being abused to reach out for help and answers than pastors? Pastors are uniquely situated to provide comfort and spiritual guidance to those who are hurting.

By looking to the Word of God, pastors can point victims to the Healer to bring the healing balm of Gilead. Pastors, when the victims are ready, can let them know that Jesus understands: He was beaten (Mark 14:65, John 18:22), whipped (Luke 22:63), betrayed (Mark 14:44), dishonored (John 8:49, Mark 15:20, John 9:34), threatened (John 7:1, Mark 14:1), deprived of justice (Acts 8:33) and finally murdered (Mark 15:24-25, John 19:33-34). Other stories in the Bible also relate abuse. Joseph, a victim of extreme jealousy, was falsely accused and imprisoned (Genesis 37 and 39). David was hounded by liars and was attacked (Psalm 109:2-5, 25). Abigail was married to an abusive man (I Samuel 25). Dinah and Tamar were raped (Genesis 34, 2 Samuel 13). The perverse men of Gibeah, offered a concubine by her husband, sexually abused her throughout the night (Judges 19). The Bible has examples of every kind of abuse. It can be comforting to a victim to know that God understands and gives us these stories to let us know He is deeply aware of the sinfulness of man.

Victim: I left my abuser several times. I had so many conflicting emotions. I was afraid. I was angry. I was hurt. I felt betrayed. I felt ashamed. I felt confused. No one in the church seemed to get it. I was told, "He's not going to kill you" as though I were a drama queen overreacting to his threats to kill me. A phone call from a mutual friend confirmed my fears when I was told, "He's going to shoot you when you get home, when you get out of the car."

Another time, a Christian couple told me, "Well, if he was drinking, that was probably why he acted that way. He's just being a guy." Weeks later my abuser pointed a gun at them while at our house. They never talked about why he acted "that way" when the danger was aimed at them.

In his article "What About All the Men?", Reverend Al Miles tells of the five questions he received from Christian males attending a conference when discussing a horrific act of violence by a Christian man against his wife. One of the questions was related to the lack of information about what the wife had done to provoke the husband's anger. The other four questions related to women abusing men. It is true that men are victims of domestic violence in 10%-15% of the reported cases. However, the violence in most of these cases is not perpetrated by women against men, but by men against men in same-sex relationships. It is also worth noting that the majority of female-toward-male violence is motivated by the woman's defense or retaliation for prior violence toward them by the male partner.[124]

What is illuminating about the responses from the men at the conference is their offering of excuses, blame-shifting, and justifications for the male abuser. This underscores the amount of work that needs to be done to correct the Church's attitude and understanding about domestic violence. Remember, abuse is not about just anger and is never the result of anything the woman has or has not done. Rather, it is willful action on the part of the abuser.

Unfortunately, there are still mindsets of some pastors that must be examined.

- *No abused women attend their church.* Failure of a woman to disclose abuse does not mean it's not happening. Statistically, it is inconceivable that of the 25% of women who are victims that some churches don't have a single victim. Remember, domestic violence is not limited to the brutal, sensationalized media portrayals.

- *Christian survivors need only God, faith, prayer, and an optimistic attitude to be freed from domestic violence.* Telling a victim to pray harder, submit more, and have more faith sends the message that the woman is responsible for her own abuse. Such advice can be potentially lethal.

- *Domestic violence only happens in urban areas and in certain racial, cultural, and socioeconomic groups.* It does not only happen to poor, uneducated minorities. It can and does happen to any woman regardless of wealth, education, culture, or background.

- *Victims can save their marriage, save their families, and stop the abuse by changing their behavior.* No woman has control over the behavior of her abuser. Abusive behavior cannot be changed by changing the victim's behavior. There is nothing wrong with her behavior. She doesn't cause the abuse– he does. The sanctity of marriage and family cannot be viewed as more important than the safety and sanctity of life.[125]

Tragically, clergy are still advising abused women to suck it up, be grateful, and try harder.

Ministering to Victims

Listening with genuine compassion and empathy for a victim's pain is the single most appreciated action you can offer. As a pastor, you are the critical listener who validates her. You are not assuming the role of investigator or judge. You patiently wait as she sorts her thoughts that may be quite jumbled after an incident. You let her tell the story in her own way, at her own speed. Be aware that you are most likely only hearing the tip of the iceberg. As you become a trusted listener over time, more of the story will unfold. However, she may never share all of her abuse with you, and that's okay.

> BE AWARE THAT YOU ARE MOST LIKELY ONLY HEARING THE TIP OF THE ICEBERG.

Victim: My story of abuse came out in pieces over time. I attended a weekly support group for several years. Bit by bit I talked about things my abuser did and said. The others in the group were so supportive and shared their experiences also. The one thing rarely talked about was the sexual abuse. Even within the group, it was an uncomfortable topic. Even after finally admitting several years later that I was sexually abused by my husband, I didn't talk about the details in group. It was just too personal, even among women who understood and had experienced it, too. It was the ultimate violation. I was too ashamed, even knowing it was not my fault. I thought people would look at me differently if they knew, so I just don't talk about it.

"Ninety-six percent of pastors say they have a responsibility to ask church members about possible abuse if they see signs of domestic or sexual violence."[126] As a pastor, act on your suspicions of abuse by talking to each party independently and away from the other. You won't know unless you ask. Her account of what happened has been proven to be more accurate than his.

> Research suggests that false reports of domestic violence are made at about the same rate as other crimes - somewhere in the neighborhood of 2% of the time. In order to make false claims of domestic violence, a woman would have to go through an extreme amount of work and inconvenience - police interviews, countless questions from friends, family, co-workers, and social service agencies, piles of paperwork to file restraining orders and stalking citations, lost time at work, attorney's fees, etc. Considering the amount of effort a woman would have to go through to lie about domestic violence, the payoff seems virtually nonexistent.[127]

Starting the Conversation

If you are concerned someone you know may be in an abusive relationship, let her know gently. "Are you okay?" Share your worry that someone is hurting her, and you are concerned for her safety. As she may be in denial about being a victim of abuse, you may want to have her take an assessment to help her see that abuse is occurring in her relationship. (See Resources 8 and 9) In a short conversation, you must be able to convey that you are going to believe her, no matter what.

The following is a list of suggested questions.

- Do you feel loved, heard, and validated in your current relationship?

- Do you feel safe in your current relationship?

- Are you in a relationship where you are yelled at, called names, or accused of something you didn't do?

- Are you in a relationship with a person who threatens you or physically hurts you?

- Who caused these injuries? (if you see bruises, cuts, scratches, or other marks)

- Have you been kicked, hit, strangled, or hurt by someone in the past year?

- Is your partner from a past relationship making you feel unsafe now?

For there is nothing covered that will not be revealed,
nor hidden that will not be. known. Therefore whatever you
have spoken in the dark will be heard in the light, and what you
have spoken in the ear in inner rooms will be proclaimed on the
housetops. Luke 12:2-3 NKJV

Listening to Disclosures of Abuse

It is often hard for pastors to reconcile the church member in the seat on Sunday with the abuser the victim is describing. These two variations of the same person can leave you feeling confused. It can be hard to believe someone just described your model church member as an abuser. Should you be trusted enough by a woman for her to share the details of her abuse with you, it is important that you use caution, especially if you are dealing with a life-threatening situation. Below is a list of principles for pastoral care of abused women as suggested by faith-based and secular organizations that provide support for abused women. (See Resource 11)

- Pray. Ask God to give her the courage and strength she needs. Pray for safety. Pray for wisdom for you both.

- Listen to her and believe her. Avoid reacting with strong emotions to what she tells you.

- Remind her that the abuse is not her fault. Abuse is never acceptable. She has the right to be safe and to make decisions that are best for her and the children, not him.

- Address concerns about injuries, be observant and listen as she may try to minimize them.

- Do not advise her to stay in or return to an unsafe environment. Place her safety above all other concerns. You can discuss specifics of the relationship later.

- Ask about her immediate needs such as childcare, food, gas money, etc.

- Help her recognize the danger to herself and her children.

- Do not minimize the danger she is in or what has happened. Do not confront the abuser without her permission and a prayerfully considered plan.

- If the situation is volatile, refer her to a shelter equipped with safety protocols. It is inadvisable to have her stay with a member of the congregation, possibly placing more people at risk.

- Do not go to a home where active violence is occurring without law enforcement or other church leaders.

- Let her know she is not alone. Refer her as soon as possible to persons or agencies that can provide appropriate resources: shelter, police response, orders of protection, safety, planning, counseling, support groups, etc.

- Do not break confidentiality! This may seem unwarranted, but if you seek additional help before she is ready, you will lose her trust and may risk her safety. Ask permission to contact a woman you or she trusts to help minister to her. Otherwise, do not tell anyone without her permission.

- Avoid spiritualizing the violence; resist the temptation to focus only on religious issues without offering practical advice.

- Keep the focus on his responsibility for his actions.

- Do not assume the marriage can be reconciled or that she wants to reconcile.

- Let her know that abuse occurs in cycles and often escalates in frequency and severity over time.

- Avoid judging her actions or lack of actions. What seems the best decision to you may not be the best decision for her. She may not reach out immediately for additional help.

- Offer her information and options, not advice. Do not make decisions for her or insist she take certain actions she is not ready to make.

- Do not recommend couple's counseling, marriage enrichment seminars, mediation, communication workshops, or any other relationship counseling.

- Stay neutral as she talks about him. Remember that it is possible and even likely that she may go back. Being impartial will help her see you as trustworthy and nonjudgmental. If you are open about your opinion of him, she may remember and assume your disapproval is about her returning to her abusive situation, making it harder for her reach out to you again.

- Remember that leaving an abuser and being safe can be a long process. Separation does not mean safety. There is no guarantee the abuse won't continue. Although it seems as if leaving will create safety, leaving actually increases her risk of danger.

- Respect her decisions, whether she decides to stay or go. Change takes time. Let her know the church will be there for her on each step of her journey.

- If she decides to stay, help her review her safety plan that involves identifying action steps to increase her safety and to prepare in advance for the possibility of further violence.

- If she decides to leave, help her mourn the loss of her relationship for herself and her children.

- If she wants to reconcile, encourage her to wait over an extended time period for signs of change in him. Repentance and forgiveness are both the work of the Holy Spirit and must operate in God's timing, not man's.

- Assure her of God's love and presence. Let her know that suffering abuse is not God's will for her life.

- Work with a team of support. Avoid her dependence on you or her establishing an emotional attachment to you.

Aftercare

Should the woman decide to leave her abuser, she will need a great deal of support from her church family. She may have left with little or nothing. She may be unable to retrieve her and her children's possessions, at least temporarily. The church can provide for immediate needs such as food, clothing, toiletries, and transportation. Long-term needs such as housing and employment can be coordinated with local organizations. Agencies dedicated to helping victims of domestic violence can also provide court advocacy, including helping with orders of protection. If criminal charges are involved, the victim advocate from the District Attorney/Prosecutor's Office may also offer support.

Court cases can take months. During that time, the abuser may try to get the victim to drop an order of protection or any charges through pressuring, threatening, or wooing. He may use the same tactics in an attempt to get her to reconcile. This period is a time of rampant and confusing emotions for the victim.

During the course of leaving and afterwards, the woman may experience a gamut of emotions:

- shock and disbelief

- denial and desperation (for understanding)

- confusion and anxiety

- bargaining and relapse (returning to relationship)

- guilt and pain

- isolation and fear

- anger and resentment

- depression and low self-esteem

- loneliness and emptiness

- uncertainty and indecision

- loss and mourning

- determination and empowerment

- acceptance and peace

- hope and expectancy

You might notice similarities to the stages of grief: denial, anger, bargaining, depression, acceptance.[128] Not everyone goes through all of the emotions, nor are the emotions in any prescribed order or limited to these five.. Victims may weave in and out of emotions and may revisit some emotions. Much like during the stages of grief, some emotions may last moments or hours; others may last days or weeks. Some emotions may last years.

WE MUST PROTECT THOSE GOD HAS ENTRUSTED TO OUR CARE.

Please understand, this woman is dealing with not only her own trauma, emotions, and loss but likely that of her children as well. She may be recovering from physical injuries. She may be maneuvering through the criminal, civil, and family court systems. She is making life-changing decisions in the midst of turmoil. She is trying to look forward while he may be trying to get her back. She is trying to survive day by day, sometimes hour by hour. What incredible strength these women have! Make sure you let these women know it is your privilege to be part of their healing journey.

It is important to remember that women do escape from violent relationships. Now is the time when we as the Church get to decide how we will respond to those victimized by domestic violence. Our support is crucial. We must protect those God has entrusted to our care. As leaders, pastors, and clergy in a community of faith, we need to educate ourselves so that we can stand in biblical truth with biblical authority against the enemy who is working to destroy God's children.

Chapter 12

The Sin of Abuse

If you hide your sins, you will not succeed. If you confess and reject them, you will receive mercy. Proverbs 28:13 NCV

When it comes to sin, we humans can try to split hairs, but sin is sin. God sees abuse as sin. The Scriptures contain over 100 condemnations of violence. There are so many variations of God rebuking stalking, lying in wait, word twisting, as well as physical, sexual, and emotional abuse. It is important that the Church recognizes abuse as sin. It must be dealt with as sin. Unrepentant abusers who do not turn from their wicked ways will not inherit the kingdom of God.

The acts of the flesh are obvious: sexual immorality, impurity and debauchery; idolatry and witchcraft; hatred, discord, jealousy, fits of rage, selfish ambition, dissensions, factions and envy; drunkenness, orgies, and the like. I warn you, as I did before, that those who live like this will not inherit the kingdom of God. Galatians 5:19-21 NIV

In Galatians 5, The Apostle Paul addresses many sins present in domestic violence relationships:

- Discord and dissension are present in every abusive home. There is a lack of harmony, unity, and peace resulting from physical or emotional abuse.

- Jealousy is an early warning indicator of an abusive personality. What appears to be loving, solicitous behavior can quickly become controlling and coercive.

- Fits of rage are used effectively by an abuser to intimidate and control his partner and children. By creating an atmosphere of fear, he gets his way.

- Drunkenness is not a cause of abuse but frequently accompanies abusive behavior. Abuser may try and use drunkenness as the reason for their abuse, but abuse is a choice. There are men that drink to excess that don't abuse and abusers who don't drink.

- Selfishness is prevalent in abusers. They believe they are entitled to act however they want whenever they want and have no consequences for their abusive behavior.

- Sexual immorality, impurity, and debauchery are frequently found in abusive relationships. Abusers have affairs, view pornography, and often sexually abuse their partners.[129]

Abusers are quick to shift the blame. The Bible also has examples of blame-shifting:

- Adam tried to shift the blame to Eve, and Eve shifted the blame to the serpent. (Genesis 3:12-13)

- Aaron who made the golden calf tried to shift the blame to the people. (Exodus 32:21-24)

- King Saul shifted the blame to the people. (1 Samuel 15:13-15)

Other domestic violence behaviors are noted in the following Scriptures:

Therefore you shall not oppress one another, but you shall fear your God; for I am the Lord your God. Leviticus 25:17 NKJV

"Then I will draw near to you for judgment. I will be a swift witness against the sorcerers, against the adulterers, against those who swear falsely, against those who oppress the hired worker in his wages, the widow and the fatherless, against those who thrust aside the sojourner, and do not fear me," says the Lord of hosts. Malachi 3:5 ESV

For out of the heart come evil thoughts and plans, murders, adulteries, sexual immoralities, thefts, false testimonies, slanders (verbal abuse, irreverent speech, blaspheming). Matthew 15:19 AMP

And He said, "Whatever comes from [the heart of] a man, that is what defiles and dishonors him. For from within, [that is] out the heart of men, come base and malevolent thoughts and schemes, acts of sexual immorality, thefts, murders, adulteries, acts of greed and covetousness, wickedness, deceit, unrestrained conduct, envy and jealousy, slander and profanity, arrogance and self-righteousness and foolishness (poor judgment)." Mark 7:20-22 AMP

And since they did not see fit to acknowledge God, God gave them up to a debased mind to do what ought not to be done. They were filled with all manner of unrighteousness, evil, covetousness, malice. They are full of envy, murder, strife, deceit, maliciousness. They are gossips, slanderers, haters of God, insolent, haughty, boastful, inventors of evil, disobedient to parents, foolish, faithless, heartless, ruthless. Though they know God's righteous decree that those who practice such things deserve to die, they not only do them but give approval to those who practice them. Romans 1:28-32 ESV

But understand this, that in the last days there will come times of difficulty. For people will be lovers of self, lovers of money, proud, arrogant, abusive, disobedient to their parents, ungrateful, unholy, heartless, unappeasable, slanderous, without self-control, brutal, not loving good, treacherous, reckless, swollen with conceit, lovers of pleasure rather than lovers of God, having the appearance of godliness, but denying its power. Avoid such people. 2 Timothy 3:1-5 ESV

Abuse Is a Heart Problem

Leslie Vernick with the Association of Biblical Counselors lists five indicators of an evil heart:

1. Evil hearts are experts at creating confusion and contention. They twist facts, mislead, lie, avoid taking responsibility, deny reality, make up stories, and withhold information.

Even from birth the wicked go astray; from the womb they are wayward, spreading lies. Psalm 58:3 NIV

A troublemaker and a villain, who goes about with a corrupt mouth who winks maliciously with his eye, signals with his feet and motions with his fingers, who plots evil with deceit in his heart— he always stirs up conflict. Proverbs 6:12-14 NIV

There are six things the Lord hates, seven that are detestable to him: haughty eyes, a lying tongue, hands that shed innocent blood, a heart that devises wicked schemes, feet that are quick to rush into evil, a false witness who pours out lies and a person who stirs up conflict in the community. Proverbs 6:16-19 NIV

Evildoers are trapped by their sinful talk, and so the innocent escape trouble. Proverbs 12:13 NIV

2. Evil hearts are experts at fooling others with their smooth speech and flattering words. But if you look at the fruit of their lives or

the follow-through of their words, you will find no real evidence of godly growth or change. It's all a façade.

> *You use your mouth for evil and harness*
> *your tongue to deceit. Psalm 50:19 NIV*

> *See what they spew from their mouths— the words*
> *from their lips are sharp as swords, and they think,*
> *"Who can hear us?" Psalm 59:7 NIV*

> *Like a coating of glaze over earthenware are fervent lips with an*
> *evil heart. The one who hates others disguises it with his lips, but*
> *he stores up deceit within him. When he speaks graciously, do not*
> *believe him, for there are seven abominations within him. Though*
> *his hatred may be concealed by deceit, his evil will be uncovered in*
> *the assembly. Proverbs 26:23–26 NET*

> *Though evil is sweet in his mouth and he hides*
> *it under his tongue. Job 20:12 NIV*

3. Evil hearts crave and demand control, and their highest authority is their own self- reference. They reject feedback, real accountability, and make their own rules to live by. They use Scriptures to their own advantage but ignore and reject passages that might require self-correction and repentance.

> *But for those who are self-seeking and who reject the truth and follow*
> *evil, there will be wrath and anger. Romans 2:8 NIV*

> *His mouth is full of cursing and deceit and oppression; under his*
> *tongue is trouble and iniquity. Psalm 10:7 KNJV*

> *Therefore pride serves as their necklace; violence covers*
> *them like a garment. Their eyes bulge with abundance;*

*they have more than heart could wish. They scoff and speak wickedly
concerning oppression; they speak loftily. They set their mouth
against the heavens, And their tongue walks
through the earth. Psalm 73:6-9 NJKV*

*The proud and arrogant person—"Mocker" is his name—
behaves with insolent fury. Proverbs 21:24 NIV*

4. Evil hearts prey on the sympathies of good-willed people, often abusing the grace card. They demand mercy but give none themselves. They demand warmth, forgiveness, and intimacy from those they have harmed with no empathy for the pain they have caused and no real intention of making amends or working toward rebuilding broken trust.

*The wicked crave evil; their neighbors get no
mercy from them. Proverbs 21:10 NIV*

*A lying tongue hates those it hurts, and a flattering
mouth works ruin. Proverbs 26:28*

*…while evildoers and imposters will go from bad to worse,
deceiving and being deceived. 2 Timothy 3:13 NIV*

*For certain individuals whose condemnation was written about long
ago have secretly slipped in among you. They are ungodly people,
who pervert the grace of our God into a license for immorality and
deny Jesus Christ our only Sovereign and Lord. Jude 1:4 NIV*

5. Evil hearts have no conscience, no remorse. They do not struggle against sin or evil. They delight in it– all the while masquerading as someone of noble character.[130]

... who delight in doing wrong and rejoice in the perverseness of evil, whose paths are crooked and who are devious in their ways. Proverbs 2:14-15 NIV

You who practice deceit, your tongue plots destruction; it is like a sharpened razor. You love evil rather than good, falsehood rather than speaking the truth. Psalm 52:2-3 NIV

A fool finds pleasure in wicked schemes, but a person of understanding delights in wisdom. Proverbs 10:23 NIV

For fools speak folly, their hearts are bent on evil: They practice ungodliness and spread error concerning the LORD; the hungry they leave empty and from the thirsty they withhold water. Isaiah 32:6 NIV

Ministering to Abusers

As a pastor, the watchman entrusted with the safety of people as noted in Ezekiel, there may come a time when you will need to confront and hold the abuser accountable. "It is important that domestic violence be recognized and dealt with as sin, because the abuser's soul is in peril."[131]

But if the watchman sees the sword coming and does not blow the trumpet to warn the people and the sword comes and takes someone's life, that person's life will be taken because of their sin, but I will hold the watchman accountable for their blood. Ezekiel 33:6 NIV

When we see a friend struggling with a problem, we are quick to focus on solutions. We want to fix things. For example, if your friend has no ride, you offer to pick him up. Then you find out his car is in the shop because he wrecked it in a fit of rage. You now are on a mission to help him control his anger. You keep him away from stressful situations that might trigger his anger. You practice deep breathing with him. You help him find calming music. You help him develop other coping skills for when he becomes angry.

However, behavior modification or applying external measures do not change the inner sin problem, the attitude of the heart, found in abusers. We are unable to change an abuser's heart, but we know the One who transforms hearts.

And I will give you a new heart, and a new spirit I will put within you. And I will remove the heart of stone from your flesh and give you a heart of flesh. And I will put my Spirit within you, and cause you to walk in my statutes and be careful to obey my rules. Ezekiel 36:26-27 ESV

When God becomes part of our lives, we are changed from the inside out. It is through the power of the Holy Spirit, the Word of God, and through prayer that our hearts and lives are changed.

All Scripture is breathed out by God and profitable for teaching, for reproof, for correction, and for training in righteousness, that the man of God may be complete, equipped for every good work. 2 Timothy 3:16-17 ESV

Therefore, confess your sins to one another and pray for one another, that you may be healed. The prayer of a righteous person has great power as it is working. James 5:16 ESV

An abusive husband disobeys Christ. Abusers do not take kindly to being confronted about their behavior, so use wisdom and proceed cautiously. As a safety precaution, it is best for you and another church leader to meet the abuser in a public place with others around. The safety of the spouse should always be the primary consideration when deciding if and when to confront the abuser. If the wife is still in the home, she may be at greater risk. It may be too dangerous for you to confront the abuser and better left to the courts, family, or professionals. However, allowing the abuser to continue to sin results in harm for the abuser and the victim.

> *... and try to discern what is pleasing to the Lord.*
> *Take no part in the unfruitful works of darkness, but instead*
> *expose them. For it is shameful even to speak of the things*
> *that they do in secret. Ephesians 5:10-12 ESV*

> *Don't hate your brother. Rebuke anyone who sins; don't let him get*
> *away with it, or you will be equally guilty. Leviticus 19:17 TLB*

Victim: I was so sure that he would stop his abuse once he quit drinking. I spent more hours reading how to help a person who abuses alcohol than I did praying for the soul of the man abusing me. I had it wrong. Without God changing him and the way he thought about his entitlements as a stronger, superior male, nothing would be different for very long.

Chapter 13

Talking with the Abuser

No one who practices deceit will dwell in my house; no one who speaks falsely will stand in my presence. Psalm 101:7 NIV

When first meeting with an abuser, with the victim's permission, it is important to determine his perception of the problem. Be prepared for skewed thinking. He may deny everything. He may admit he has a problem but minimize his actions and the effects of his actions. He may claim she or the kids are the ones with the problem. He may say he has the same relationship problems as everyone else. When asking the following questions, avoid his attempts to generalize his behavior: other people's partners act that way too, or all women/men act that way sometimes. Keep the focus on his attitudes and behavior. Refuse to accept any abusive behavior aimed at you. Do not allow him to de-personalize his partner; insist she be called by name.

Ask:

• Does your partner seem nervous around you?

• Does your partner seem afraid of you?

- Does your partner move away from you when you're angry?

- Does your partner cry because you make her do something or won't let her do something?

- Does your partner seem scared or unable to express opinions or disagree with you?

- Does your partner confine her interactions with others to ones that please you?

- Do you feel possessive or insecure about your partner's relationships with others?

- Do you often check up on your partner or have your partner check in with you through calls and texts?

- Does your partner need to ask your permission before spending time with others, getting a job, or going to school?

- Do you get angry when your partner doesn't do what you want or act the way you want?

- Do you have a hard time controlling your anger and calming down when you are angry?

- Have you ever blamed your partner for your anger?

- Have you ever blamed your anger on drugs and/or alcohol?

- Have you ever called your partner names or said demeaning things when you were angry?

- Have you ever threatened to hurt or have physically hurt your partner when you were angry?

- Does your partner have to come to you for money for any purchases?

- Do you require your partner to prove where money was spent?

- Do you force your partner to be intimate with you?[132]

Lies Abusers Frequently Tell

*So put away all malice and all deceit and hypocrisy
and envy and all slander. 1 Peter 2:1 ESV*

Since abusers are prone to lying, excusing, and shifting blame, these common lies are told to victims and those confronting the abuser with the abuse. Expect to hear these lies as you talk to the abuser.

- I just need to be understood.

- I had a bad childhood.

- I have no control over it.

- She's the one who is abusive, or she is abusive too.

- I have to control her, so she doesn't control me.

- When I destroy things, I'm not being abusive; I'm venting.

- I have a lot of stress in my life.

- I'm not abusive; I just have an anger problem.

- I only act that way when I drink or do drugs.

- You have no idea what she is really like.

- I'm not the one with the problem.

- If she would just... or, If she wouldn't...[133]

"An abuser is a human being, not an evil monster, but he has a profoundly complex and destructive problem that should not be underestimated ... An abuser's behavior is primarily conscious–he acts deliberately rather than by accident or by losing control of himself–but the underlying thinking that drives his behavior is largely not conscious ... He knows what he is doing but not necessarily why."[134]

Cautions When Talking with Abusers

Break the arm [strip the power] of the wicked and the evil man!
Hold him accountable for his wicked deeds, which he thought
you would not discover. Psalm 10:15 NET

Beware, abusers are master manipulators. Get ready for it. Don't underestimate their powers of persuasion, logic, and deceit. Most have been manipulating a long time. Logic and rational thinking don't work with them because they don't really believe that what they're doing is wrong. They may be convinced they are the victims. Even if they tell you they see that it's wrong, they are just saying what they know you want to hear. They truly believe they are entitled to act the way they do. They may try to justify and rationalize their abuse. They may try to suck you into believing the victim is the real problem and divert conversations into discussions of the victim's behavior. They will try to tell you the victim is exaggerating or try to minimize the abuse. They will seek the sympathy of others in the church. They will attempt to enlist you and other church leaders as allies. Abusers will passionately deny they are abusive. They do not want their behavior to become public knowledge. They will go to incredible lengths to get supporters, often convincingly portraying themselves as falsely accused.

- Abusers will divide and conquer by telling different versions of the facts to different people in an effort to create division.

- Instead of admitting responsibility, expect the abuser to spend a lot of energy trying to enlist you as an ally.

- Abusers may appear righteously angry, constantly challenging you as a tactic to get you to back off, thereby avoiding account-ability and providing him opportunity to pressure his partner into returning. It is best to leave or terminate any conversation when anger or other emotions escalate beyond what is reasonable.

- Abusers may be overly accommodating and appear to be in complete control as they try to "clear up this misunderstanding." He may suggest he and his wife work on the problem together, giving him access to her once again.

- Men who abuse love arguments and battles for dominance. Do not engage in arguments; keep discussions impersonal. Focus on options and consequences.

- Abusers may try to get you to divulge what their partners have said. Do not share any information without the victim's permission and without full assessment of the potential risk to the victim.[135]

The more you try to reason with abusers and show them mercy, the more you become part of the game they are playing. They want you to tell them their horrendous behavior is excused from serious or painful consequences. They expect by saying, "I'm sorry" that all is forgiven. They expect grace to be offered and the slate wiped clean, regardless of the wake of trauma they left behind them. They will pressure you to advocate on their behalf for reconciliation. "Can't we just let this go?"

THEY EXPECT GRACE TO BE OFFERED AND THE SLATE WIPED CLEAN, REGARDLESS OF THE WAKE OF TRAUMA THEY LEFT BEHIND THEM.

Smooth words may hide a wicked heart, just as a pretty glaze covers a clay pot. People may cover their hatred with pleasant words, but they're deceiving you. They pretend to be kind, but don't believe them. Their hearts are full of many evils. While their hatred may be concealed by trickery, their wrongdoing will be exposed in public.
Proverbs 26:23-26 NLT

He may talk the talk of a man who believes the Scripture, can often rattle off plenty of verses, but his walk doesn't match his talk. Over time, it is prudent to question his relationship with God. It is important not to collude with the abuser and pressure the victim to forgive, forget, and to trust again when there is no evidence of any real, heartfelt change in him. Don't be surprised when he stops coming to you when you continue to confront his sin. It is better he knows his sin will not be overlooked, minimized, or accepted where you are the pastor.

Avoiding Re-victimization

One of the ways victims of abuse are re-victimized is by participating in couples counseling together. The main problem with this type of counseling is the implication that both partners are at fault in the relationship. Abuse is not a relationship problem; the choice to abuse falls fully on the abuser. Unwitting therapists who are unaware of the abuse may actually reinforce the behaviors and attitudes of the abuser, leading to escalation. By focusing on improving communication or relationship issues, the abusive behaviors are never properly addressed.

ABUSE IS NOT A RELATIONSHIP PROBLEM; THE CHOICE TO ABUSE FALLS FULLY ON THE ABUSER.

"Couples counseling can end up being a big setback for the abused woman. The more she insists that her partner's cruelty or intimidation needs to be addressed, the more she may find the therapist looking down at her saying, 'It seems like you are determined to put all the blame on him and are refusing to look at your part in this.' The therapist thereby inadvertently echoes the abuser's attitude, and the woman is forced to deal with yet another context in which she must defend herself, which is the last thing she needs."[136]

Another way a victim is re-victimized is by failing to hold abusers accountable so little or no consequences are meted out. I have heard too many stories about abusers who have convinced the police that it was the victim doing the abusing, and the victim was the one arrested. I have heard too many stories where the judge believed him when he said he wouldn't do it again and was released. I have heard too many stories where he convinced his counselor his wife had mental problems, so he won custody of the children. These stories go on and on. It's hard to believe that one man could fool so many people, and yet he does. These are men who have manipulated law enforcement officers, attorneys, counselors, parole officers, and judges as well as their victims, often avoiding consequences for their actions. As pastors, it is important you do not allow them to manipulate you.

"Holding abusers fully responsible means refusing to accept any excuses or minimizations for violence whatsoever. If clergy accept abusers' blame-shifting or minimizations, this inevitably serves as stronger reinforcement for the abusers' pathological beliefs and actions. It is also profoundly harmful to battered wives."[137]

Victim: I had just left court after getting an order of protection. Truly, I hadn't even driven a mile when my phone rang. "Do you want to go get some breakfast?" I was floored. He had just assured the judge he wouldn't contact me, even signed a paper saying he would stay away, and here he was calling me within five minutes wanting me to meet him. I really thought I was safe. I really thought he would honor the court papers. It never occurred to me he would lie to a judge.

The Abuser and Repentance

But we have renounced disgraceful, underhanded ways. We refuse to practice cunning or to tamper with God's word, but by the open statement of the truth we would commend ourselves to everyone's conscience in the sight of God. 2 Corinthians 4:2 ESV

Victim: One time I left and actually got another place to live. I had proof he had cheated so he couldn't deny it. I had a Biblical reason to leave– adultery– and took it. After two weeks, I got a phone call from his mother at my work. She told me it wasn't right for me not to answer his calls. He was so worried not knowing where I was. It wasn't fair for me to keep his child from him. I felt guilty so I answered his call that night. He came over and was quite contrite. He talked about forgiveness and turning the other cheek. He said he made a mistake and wanted nothing more than for his family to be together. It wouldn't happen again. I believed his promises. I wanted to believe his promises. I went back to him and lived with his abuse another 10 years. I often wondered how my life and my child's life would have been different if I had never gone back.

The difficulty for victims and pastors is determining if the abuser is filled with temporary regret and remorse as was Judas after betraying Jesus (Matthew 27:3) or experiencing a true change of heart and deep sorrow for his sin as did David (Psalms 32 and 51). Has he expressed godly sorrow which leads to true repentance?

For the kind of sorrow God wants us to experience leads us away from sin and results in salvation. There's no regret for that kind of sorrow. But worldly sorrow, which lacks repentance, results in spiritual death. 2 Corinthians 7:10 NLT

If it is discerned that the abuser is truly repentant and has a sincere heartfelt desire to change, it is still good to remember there is no quick fix. There is no easy cure. He has been in the clutches of the enemy for much of his life. He most likely has been abusive for years so he should expect years of hard work ahead of him. Change will require full commitment on his part.

This course of action isn't about stopping drinking or cheating or learning how to control his anger. It is about changing his core belief system of entitlement and selfishness. It's about changing his attitude and behavior toward women.

*Blessed is the one who finds wisdom, and the one
who gets understanding. Proverbs 3:13 ESV*

Here are some expectations:

- Make a full disclosure of all his abuse toward any current or past partners.
- Feel deeply ashamed for his sinful behavior and address the underlying spiritual condition that needs attention.
- Admit his abuse is a sin against God and his family and is unconditionally wrong.
- Fully admit his actions were wrong and stop blaming her or the children.
- Show empathy for the effects of his actions on his partner and children.
- Stop justifying, rationalizing, and making excuses for what he has done.
- Identify patterns of controlling behaviors and entitlement attitudes.
- Take full responsibility for his actions and make amends/restitution.
- Admit that abuse is a choice and there is no "cure."
- Accept the consequences for his actions within the church, his home, and the legal system.
- Develop kind, supportive, respectful attitudes and behaviors toward women.
- Share his power and carry his weight.
- Change how he responds to intense conflict.
- Change how he parents and treats her as a parent.
- Change how he responds to his partner's anger and grievances.

- Avoid expecting his progress to be conditional on his partner getting help.

- Seek professionals to help understand the deeply embedded, distorted thinking behind his actions.

- Wait willingly for those he hurt to rebuild trust or accept that reconciliation is not going to happen.

- Participate successfully in specialized programs designed for abusers.

- Participate successfully in additional programs to deal with addiction or other side issues.

- Avoid expecting any abusive act to be tolerated, no matter how much progress he has made.

- Commit to becoming the man of God, husband, and father he is meant to be.

- Accept that a significant amount of time needs to pass where there is no further abuse (at least a year from onset of treatment) validated separately by his partner before reconciliation is discussed.[138]

Therefore bear fruits worthy of repentance, Matthew 3:8 NKJV

Even so, every good tree bears good fruit, but a bad tree bears bad fruit. A good tree cannot bear bad fruit, nor can a bad tree bear good fruit. Every tree that does not bear good fruit is cut down and thrown into the fire. Therefore by their fruits you will know them. Matthew 7:17-20 NKJV

Confronting the Sin of Abuse in the Church

"Providing nurturing concern and healing resources is an appropriate response for victims of violence. However, for perpetrators, the most loving response may be the development of systems of accountability and consequences that stop their destructive behaviors."[139]

Galatians and Matthew both provide instructions for what to do if a typical believer is overtaken by sin.

Brethren, if a man is overtaken in any trespass, you who are spiritual restore such a one in a spirit of gentleness, considering yourself lest you also be tempted. Galatians 6:1 NKJV

If one of my followers sins against you, go and point out what was wrong. But do it in private, just between the two of you. If that person listens, you have won back a follower. But if that one refuses to listen, take along one or two others. The Scriptures teach that every complaint must be proven true by two or more witnesses. If the follower refuses to listen to them, report the matter to the church. Anyone who refuses to listen to the church must be treated like an unbeliever or a tax collector. Matthew 18:15-17 CEV

- The mature should use gentleness to try and restore him.

- Privately go to him.

- If the believer refuses to listen, take along one or two more so there are two or more witnesses.

- If the believer still refuses to listen, report the matter back to the church.

- Anyone who refuses to listen to the church is to be treated as an outsider.

However, should it be determined a believer has a lifestyle of abusive behavior, the Apostle Paul gives clear directions about how the Church should handle such evil in 1 Corinthians 5. He doesn't talk about handling the sin the same as in Matthew 18, but the need to purge and disassociate from unrepentant perpetrators within the Church.

When I wrote to you before, I told you not to associate with people who indulge in sexual sin. But I wasn't talking about unbelievers who indulge in sexual sin, or are greedy, or cheat people, or worship idols. You would have to leave this world to avoid people like that. I meant that you are not to associate with anyone who claims to be a believer yet indulges in sexual sin, or is greedy, or worships idols, or is abusive, or is a drunkard, or cheats people. Don't even eat with such people. It isn't my responsibility to judge outsiders, but it certainly is your responsibility to judge those inside the church who are sinning. God will judge those on the outside; but as the Scriptures say, "You must remove the evil person from among you."
1 Corinthians 5:9-13 NLT

- Stop the fellowship with them.

- Judge them.

- Remove the person from the church setting.

The purpose is not punishment but remediation so that the Christian in sin returns to fellowship with God.

You are to deliver this man to Satan for the destruction of the flesh, so that his spirit may be saved in the day of the Lord.
1 Corinthians 5:5 ESV

Carol Adams, author of *Woman Battering*, offers this suggested conversation with abusers:

"I am on your side as you become a person who does not batter. I am against your battering behavior. I do not believe you should treat your wife as an object that can be battered. But I am in total support of you as you seek to change. I am calling you to repent and to change. You will probably suffer in the process of change. You cannot rely on old coping mechanisms that include battering. New life is possible, but it requires work."[140]

Addressing Domestic Violence with Your Congregation

As a pastor, you have many opportunities to address domestic violence with your congregation. You want to send an affirming message to those who have experienced abuse that your body of believers is united in its views and policies for addressing relationship abuse.

- Condemn violence from the pulpit.

- Be a voice for all the victims openly praying for those living with violence in the home.

- Discuss your church's zero tolerance for violence in the home during pre-marital counseling sessions.

- Create marital vows that affirm nonviolence.

- Have youth leaders address healthy relationship and relationship violence with teens, the earlier the better.

- Provide a display for information about domestic violence and resources in a safe place for her to access, such as on a door in a restroom stall.

- Let the word out that any church under your leadership is a sanctuary for those who are abused.

- Collaborate with and seek help from community agencies for those who disclose violence in the home.

- Partner with community agencies that offer support and advocacy for victims.

- Offer spiritual guidance to women in shelters who request it.

- Raise up your flock to care for those who are wounded and hurting until they thrive and grow.

- Offer support groups within the church to minister to victims.

- Offer meeting space for domestic violence weekly support groups and provide childcare.

- Hold abusers accountable.

- Develop protocols addressing abuse situations. Dialogue with fellow clergy about the challenges of ministering to parties involved in domestic violence situations.

- Sponsor conferences and trainings on violence against teens and women.

- Donate financially to domestic violence programs and community projects.

- Attend domestic violence awareness and education events in the community (October is Domestic Violence Awareness Month).[141]

"When abuse happens in church families, everyone should understand that there cannot be an instantaneous solution. Situations that developed over years cannot be addressed in a day. It is always easier to look the other way than to demand redress for evil, but to this God has summoned us, and we must shoulder the responsibility for problems that we in part have helped to create. If we have tolerated a shocking situation in our midst, we must pray, study, and act to right the wrong."[142]

If my people who are called by my name humble themselves,
and pray and seek my face and turn from their wicked ways,
then I will hear from heaven and will forgive their sin
and heal their land. 2 Chronicles 7:14 ESV

Chapter 14

Small Groups for Survivors of Domestic Violence

*And so it was, when Moses held up his hand, that Israel prevailed;
and when he let down his hand, Amalek prevailed. But Moses' hands
became heavy; so they took a stone and put it under him, and he sat
on it. And Aaron and Hur supported his hands, one on one side, and
the other on the other side; and his hands were steady until the going
down of the sun. Exodus 17:11-12 NKJV*

"Forty percent of adults in the United States claim membership in a
small group for regular support and care. Roughly seventy-five million
Americans find strength in a small group source. This means there are
approximately three million groups in existence, averaging one group
for every eighty persons living in the United States today."[143]

You may be thinking, "I know how to lead a small group. This is not
my first time." All your experience as a veteran leader will definitely
help you on this new journey. Keep in mind that leading a small group
for victims of domestic violence is a bit different from leading other
groups. You may experience anger, frustration, fear, and dismay. You
may find an overpowering need to rescue or to distance yourself from

the participants. You may find your own beliefs about domestic violence, abusers, and/or survivors challenged. You may have issues arise from your own past that must be addressed. You may realize that you need to reach out for help yourself before you can help others. You may laugh, cry, rejoice, and grieve all in one session.

You may be thinking, "I don't know how to lead this small group." Too often we convince ourselves that God can't use us to make a difference. You think these women are too broken. They need more help than you can give. You are right– they are broken, but our God specializes in healing the broken.

> *He heals the brokenhearted and binds up their wounds.*
> *Psalm 147:3 ESV*

The help they need comes from God. The help you need to lead this group comes from God. You are His vessel. When you realize the burden is on Him, not you, it makes it easier to agree to be a part of this ministry.

> *I lift up my eyes to the hills. From where does*
> *my help come? My help comes from the Lord,*
> *who made heaven and earth. Psalm 121:1-2 ESV*

You will be listening to the traumatic experiences that have led these beloved ladies to this small group. It is important that you focus on the incredible strength and capabilities of these remarkable women. The women in this group may be at all stages of their journey with abuse:

- They left the relationship long ago.
- They are still in their abusive relationship.
- They are thinking about leaving the relationship.
- They recently left the relationship.

- They are thinking about returning to the relationship.

- They just returned to the relationship.

- The relationship just became abusive.

Your success is not based on whether or not a woman leaves her abuser. Your success is measured by the growth in her relationship with Christ. You will be fostering the ability to discover and define who these incredible women are in Christ, help them understand and accept the love of God, to believe and receive the healing power of God, and to identify and overcome hindrances that keep them from being the woman of destiny God called them to be. You will be encouraging them in a personal, intimate relationship with Jesus Christ. What a privilege we have been given!

> YOUR SUCCESS IS NOT BASED ON WHETHER OR NOT A WOMAN LEAVES HER ABUSER. YOUR SUCCESS IS MEASURED BY THE GROWTH IN HER RELATIONSHIP WITH CHRIST.

Most local, state, and national organizations have a minimum number of hours of training required before volunteers and staff engage in direct interactions with victims of domestic violence. I am not suggesting you receive hours upon hours of training; however, leaders do need to understand domestic violence is a complex pattern of behavior with victims employing a variety of survival strategies. Even with training, until you've walked in her shoes, you can't truly understand her life. However, what you can offer is Christ-centered, loving support.

"Through my early years counseling battered women, I learned that the level of support coming from a woman's family or friends strongly impacted how successful she was at gaining lasting freedom from abuse."[144]

Small Group Goals

In ministering to victims who have suffered abuse, our priorities will be a bit different from other groups.

- First, ensure safety, not just for the victims but the other participants including the leaders. Although you want to attract those who sincerely are interested, the title of your group should never publicly mention domestic violence, victims, abuse, or any other identifying words. Safety is two-fold: physical safety and emotional safety. Meet in rooms with doors that close, walls thick enough that voices can't be overheard, and covered windows to ensure safety and privacy.

- Second, empower the victims toward physical, emotional, and spiritual healing and wholeness by understanding who God is, who they are in Him, and applying His Word to their lives.

- Third, encourage each woman to participate, grow, and encourage others.

- Fourth, allow change to happen by the leading of the Holy Spirit through the power of God.

Do not conform to the pattern of this world, but be transformed by the renewing of your mind. Then you will be able to test and approve what God's will is—his good, pleasing and perfect will. Romans 12:2 NIV

God as a Protector of Women

Who will rise up for me against the wicked? Who will take a stand for me against evildoers? Psalm 94:16 NIV

Women of faith have a tremendous struggle deciding to leave a marriage, even if she is being abused. She has read the Scripture about God hating divorce. She has been told there are only two reasons for divorce. She has read that a marriage after divorce makes her an adulterer and considers a future being forever single. She has heard the "turn the other cheek" and "forgive seventy times seven" sermons. She repeatedly repents for thinking any negative thoughts about her husband or thinking how much easier it would be if one of them just died. She has been so submissive her shoulders are perpetually bowed, and not just to God. Her prayer life would put many to shame. It is an insult to suggest she needs to try harder!

Victim: As a Christian in an abusive marriage, my life was a life of fasting and continual prayer. I cried out to God day and night. I meditated on the Word, praying for the "key" to making my marriage work. I spent hours on my face before God praying over my marriage and my husband. I sought wisdom from Christian people I knew, but no one could really make that decision to say, "Enough!" but me. I agonized over wanting to please God and be in His will and desiring to be free from a life of abuse. I wanted to be that godly wife found in Scripture. I worked so hard at it! I never stopped trying. The enemy, even now years later, tries to get me thinking I should have done more.

THE CHURCH MUST TAKE ITS ROLE IN SHAPING HEALTHY FAMILIES SERIOUSLY.

The women of faith I know who experience partner abuse put much more effort into making their marriages work than most outsiders know. Their application of the Scriptures to their relationship generally comes from the spiritual authority of their church. If those spiritual authorities have not fully studied the Scriptures on abuse, divorce and remarriage, if they don't have knowledge and training in responding to domestic violence, they may be condemning a woman and her children to a life of hell on earth…or even death. The Church must take its role in shaping healthy families seriously.

My people will live in peaceful dwelling places, in secure homes,
in undisturbed places of rest. Isaiah 32:18 NIV

Why Small Groups?

Two are better than one, because they have a good reward for their
toil. For if they fall, one will lift up his fellow. But woe to him who is
alone when he falls and has not another to lift him up! Again, if two
lie together, they keep warm, but how can one keep warm alone? And
though a man might prevail against one who is alone,
two will withstand him—a threefold cord is not quickly broken.
Ecclesiastes 4:9-12 ESV

What is it that draws a woman to a small group? Although many secular groups can and do provide excellent support for victims of domestic violence, they are usually bound by the guidelines of their funding provider. There is little or no freedom to lead discussions involving the name of Jesus. In contrast, everything we do as the Church in this ministry is viewed through the lens of Christianity. Jesus offers victims what the world cannot– peace and wholeness.

I have told you these things, so that in Me you may have [perfect]
peace. In the world you have tribulation and distress and suffering,
but be courageous [be confident, be undaunted, be filled with joy]; I
have overcome the world." [My conquest is accomplished,
My victory abiding.] John 16:33 AMP

The Lord will give strength to His people; The Lord will bless
His people with peace. Psalm 29:11 NKJV

In the New Testament, the word *peace* is the Strong's Greek Lexicon Number 1515 for the Greek word *Eirene* meaning peace, harmony, tranquility, safety, welfare, health. Additionally, in the Old Testament, the Strong's Greek Lexicon corresponds *Eirene* to the Hebrew word *Shalom*. According to Strong's Hebrew Lexicon Number 7965, *Shalom* means peace, safety, prosperity, well-being, intactness, wholeness.[145]

"God is able to free us from our past … This freedom experienced in and through Jesus Christ enables a person to journey onward, looking to the future rather than the past."[146]

Jim Collins explains the difference between worldly positive thinking and the faith of a believer:

> Positive thinking is similar to what God calls "faith." However, positive thinking is limited by the abilities of the individual. Faith has no limits because God has no limits. Faith allows an individual to tap into the force that created the universe. Positive thinking begins and ends with the human mind. Faith is a product of the human spirit. Positive thinking attempts to attain happiness as a result of thinking positive thoughts. Faith provides joy in all circumstances. Positive thinking focuses on positive thoughts. Faith thinks according to the Word of God. Positive thinking hopes to possess the objects of its thoughts. Faith possesses the rights, privileges, and benefits that God has already provided. Positive thinking gives credit to man. Faith gives glory to God. Positive thinking strives to win in life based on the ability to maintain a positive attitude. Faith has already secured the victory and responds to the circumstances in life with thanksgiving.[147]

Our psychological well-being requires us to be with others. Isolating ourselves from others leads us to develop in unhealthy ways. We want to belong. Our relationships with others help influence our sense of identity and worth. Feeling loved makes life worth living. We want to matter to someone; it gives our lives meaning and purpose.

Knowing that we are not alone, that others struggle as we do, brings a sense of freedom, comfort, and peace.[148] "People join small groups for both personal and corporate benefit. Our well-being as individuals and also as a local church body is enhanced as we meet together and discuss things that will improve the way we live and how we relate to those around us."[149]

First, the woman comes for support. She wants unconditional love and acceptance. She will be alert for any signs of rejection, blame, shame, or spiritual abuse. Unfortunately, not all churches advise women in domestic violence situations with a proper understanding of abuse and proper application of the Scripture.

Second, the woman progresses to where she desires growth. She wants a better life for herself and her children. She wants to be the woman God says she is, not the woman the abuser says she is. She may take one step forward and two steps backward, but she will resolve to make changes in her life with the help of her supporters and the power of God.

Third, the woman is committed to new life, a life of peace and joy firmly rooted in her relationship with God. Whatever challenges come her way she knows she does not have to go through it alone.

Fourth, the woman has experienced healing and wholeness herself and wants to offer a helping hand to others. Out of her own experiences, she can share her journey with others, offering hope and a new way of living.[150]

Blessed be the God and Father of our Lord Jesus Christ,
the Father of mercies and God of all comfort, who comforts
us in all our affliction, so that we may be able to comfort those
who are in any affliction, with the comfort with which we ourselves
are comforted by God. 2 Corinthians 1:3-4 ESV

People yearn for a sense of connectedness to other people and God. The Church body offers a sense of community often missing in today's families. "Family and friends continue to be as influential in the lives of abuse victims as they have ever been. They are still usually the ones on the front line, the first to learn of the abuse, and the first responders."[151]

We have a biblical mandate as well as a moral obligation to meet the needs of individuals through unconditional love, acceptance, and grace. Small groups afford the opportunity to make connections. Small groups that offer support and a sense of connectedness are also proven to help people develop new patterns of behavior.[152] James Houston suggests that, "the depth of intimacy in human relationships is what will bring depth to the relationship with God."[153]

According to the survivors I have interviewed, among the most important characteristics of small group leaders were: truly listening, validating experiences and emotions, showing genuine compassion, withholding judgement, creating a sense of family, and offering hope. As Christians, who among us do not possess these abilities?

Hope deferred makes the heart sick, but a desire
fulfilled is a tree of life. Proverbs 13:12 ESV

Core Beliefs

With any group, you want to promote unity within the group. It is helpful to start with a core set of beliefs. All should expect to agree. Here are some suggested core beliefs to share with the group periodically:

- God is our healer. Through a relationship with Him, we are changed.

- Only the abuser is responsible for abuse. Nothing the victim did or didn't do caused the abuse.

- There is no excuse for abuse. No abuse is acceptable or justifiable.

- We cannot change anyone's thoughts or actions but our own. We are only responsible for our own progress.

- Abuse is about the power and control of one person over another through fear and manipulation.

- Every woman's journey is different, even if commonalities exist.

- Abuse affects everyone: family, friends, co-workers, communities, and the Church.

- Women and children deserve to live free of abuse. It is God's will.

Common Expectations

It is also helpful to establish common expectations for the group. It is helpful to review them with the group when each new member joins. We are here to empower her as a woman and a child of God while acknowledging that her pain is real.

"The physical and emotional experience of pain is processed throughout the whole brain, but specifically in three major areas. In females, these areas are all bigger than in males causing women to experience pain more intensely."[154] While this is true, "God has designed you with special abilities to cope with extreme circumstances, but you weren't created to live in a state of constant trauma and crisis. You were wired for love."[155]

- All women will be believed, respected, and trusted. Our words, tone, and body language will reflect these attitudes. Our experiences and emotions will be validated.

- We will build each other up as sisters in Christ, encouraging a closer walk with God.

- We may offer alternate ways of looking at things but will refrain from giving unsolicited advice, taking unsolicited action, or compelling a direction.
  - Avoid "You should…" or "You shouldn't have…" statements.

- Avoid "What I think you should do is…" or "You didn't ask me but …" or "Wouldn't it have been better if…" statements.
- Avoid "I did _____ for you" or "You need to…"

• Each person will have an opportunity and be encouraged to share. Sharing will be based on each person's own experiences.

• Only one person will share at a time. Avoid side conversations and interruptions. For women who have been silenced and have had opinions and emotions dismissed, interruptions and side conversations further the idea that what she has to say is unimportant and not worth taking the time to hear.

• We will establish and respect group and individual boundaries.

• No legal advice will be given. We are not qualified.

• Confidentiality will be enforced. Violators will be terminated from the group.

• We will show respect for each other by arriving on time, attending consistently, and eliminating distractions (such as cell phones).

The following poem is a beautiful reminder that our ministry is to help empower women.

We Are Here

We are here to listen …Not to work miracles.
We are here to help a woman discover what she is feeling …
Not to make her feelings go away.
We are here to help a woman identify her options …
Not to decide for her what she should do.
We are here to discuss steps with a woman …
Not to take steps for her.
We are here to help a woman discover her own strength …
Not to rescue her and leave her still vulnerable.

We are here to help a woman discover she can help herself ...
Not to take responsibility for her.
We are here to help a woman learn to choose ...
Not to keep her from making difficult choices.
We are here to provide support for change.

– Anonymous[156]

Guidelines for Leaders

Listed below are suggested guidelines specific to leaders working with victims of abuse.

- The leaders must have a clear understanding of Scripture and be able to explain its meaning and application for our lives. They must be able to locate specific Scriptures using reference tools such as a concordance. Many ladies to whom I have ministered have little or no knowledge of how to use the Bible, so be prepared to give lessons in Bible use fundamentals.

- The leaders must have a clear knowledge of domestic violence dynamics. I do suggest also connecting with your local, state, and national domestic violence organizations.

- The leaders need to have a working knowledge of group dynamics to ensure respectful and purposeful discussions.

- There should always be at least two leaders.
    - Leaders work together alternating leading and supporting throughout the lesson.
    - Should one leader have an expected absence, the other leader will be available to fill in. Victims of domestic violence struggle with trusting others so continuity within the group is vital.
    - It is also possible a woman will need one-on-one support during the group, and the leader will be able to accommo-

date the victim's need while the other leader continues with the group.

- Having two people in a leadership role is also important because the information shared in the group must remain confidential among all the participants. While confidentiality is suggested in all small groups, it is crucial and mandatory for groups involving victims of domestic violence. The danger is real should the right information get to the wrong person. The participants will appreciate the zero tolerance for breaking confidentiality. It is her story to tell, no one else's. Even if no names are mentioned, identifying information might be enough to put the woman in danger. For example, if you were to say, "That young mom with the twins is so sweet. I can't believe all she's been through," you have just passed along information about her age, she's a mother, she has twins, and that you know her. It wouldn't take much effort in most churches to find out who you are, what ministry you provide, and the time and location of the ministry. Never underestimate the determination and cunning of an abuser. You may have just jeopardized your safety, her safety, and the safety of the group.

- Because of strict confidentiality, the leaders will be able to discuss what happens during the small group only with each other and no one else, unless prior permission is given by the participants. You will want to check with your church leadership regarding mandated reporting of child abuse and the duty-to-inform mandate.

- Prayer requests are confidential and must remain within the group. While it is the nature of most churches to have as many as possible pray for a need, the needs expressed in the group need to be prayed for in the group. Hopefully, the church prayer team will be lifting up prayers throughout the small group sessions for safety and wholeness in Christ for all the women and leaders.

- Leaders should be sensitive to the pace of healing for each woman. Each may be trying as hard as she can to climb this mountain called healing. Some may race quickly to the top; others may find taking a single step is all she can handle. It does no good for others who are ahead to keep telling her to try harder or telling her what she needs to do. She is trying. Rather than continue to remind her how far behind she is or how far she still has to go, all should walk alongside her at her pace, so no one is left behind.

- Leaders should know their limitations. They should know when they are out of their depth and be willing to reach out for help. We all have strengths and challenges. We all have our own unique giftings and callings. We all have our own realm of knowledge and experiences. We are one body working together for the benefit of the group members.

- The leaders and group members must only be women. Women are more likely to participate and feel comfortable if the group is comprised of just women. It goes beyond the ministry adage: men minister to men and women minister to women. These women have been hurt by men and are still healing from the damage done by a man (or in some instances, men). In addition, victims of domestic violence need role models of Christ- empowered women.

- Children are not allowed in the group. Childcare should be offered when possible. Caring for children in a nearby room is ideal, but children should be far enough away that moms won't be distracted by kid sounds, and kids can't hear what is shared. The mothers need time away from their children to be part of the group but can become anxious if their children are not close by. Children may experience similar anxiety being too far away from Mom.

- Flexibility is a must. Sometimes the Holy Spirit will have a different plan for the lesson. Sometimes a lesson will take much longer than expected due to the amount of healing taking place. Sometimes, a woman might have a desperate need to be heard and the lesson is never touched. Remember, the Holy Spirit is in charge. This ministry should never be about our agenda or covering a chapter a week.

Structuring Small Groups

Victim: The first time I walked into a small group for survivors, I was a mess: I couldn't stop shaking, I couldn't sit still, I cried a lot, and I had trouble concentrating. At first, I didn't say anything but my first name. The leader and other participants never pushed me to say more. They just welcomed me, told me how brave I was to walk into that room, and slid the tissue box my way. As I heard what brought other women to the group, I realized I wasn't the only one. Other women could actually relate to what I experienced. They understood my overwhelming fear, my sense of helplessness, and my feelings of hopelessness. They helped me understand it wasn't my fault. They helped me understand there was nothing I could do if he didn't want to change. They helped me understand the cycle of violence and why I was hooked into going back each time. They gave me material to read, little of it faith-based. They helped me get strong enough to end an 18-year relationship of abuse. As much as my family and friends tried to understand and help, they just couldn't. These women could and did. The one thing I would have liked to have was the bigger faith component. I wanted someone to pray with me, help me find Scriptures to read, help me work through my feelings and doubt with the Bible as my guide. I wish God could have been in more of the conversations.

Although no two small groups will be the same, Julie Gorman identifies seven components of highly effective small groups.

- **Purpose** A clear statement of the purpose of the group and what it will accomplish is needed.

- **Commitment** Expectations and responsibilities for the group need to be clearly communicated:
    a. Frequency of meeting
    b. Attendance expectations
    c. Outside of group requirements [For victims of abuse, I would not expect any.]
    d. Confidentiality
    e. Accountability

- **Size** The smaller the group, the greater the opportunity for participation. A greater possibility exists for group involvement and discussion with groups numbering between five and eight participants.

- **Configuration** Arrange seating at a distance and in a manner that is comfortable for the participants. Being too far or too close to one another can cause discomfort. I have found what works best for my ladies is sitting around a table, preferably a round one.

- **Timing** The more often the group meets, the greater likelihood a participant will trust and open up to the others. The length of time spent together also impacts group dynamics. Groups meeting a minimum of 90 minutes experience greater cohesion. The more fellowship–including eating and recreation–the quicker the bonding process.

- **Leadership style** Leadership is perhaps the most important component of a small group. The leader's role, personality, leadership style, and amount of experience will influence the effectiveness of the group. Leaders will need to be flexible as the dynamics of the group changes and the group members become empowered.

- **Climate** The group members decide the spoken and unspoken standards of the group. Groups can be open, which means new members can be added at any time; closed, which means the group is set for a specified time period and includes only those who were present at the beginning; or a combination in which the group can be open at the beginning and closed after a few sessions to allow for stability of the group.[157]

Leading a group of victims of domestic violence is distinct from other groups. The key is establishing trusting, safe relationships. The leader and the participants will be tested. An abused woman tends to be isolated, suspicious, fearful, and unpredictable.[158] She will be reading your signals to determine if you are a safe person with whom she can share. She fears not being believed, being judged, having her experience minimized, and having to make changes. Connecting with each victim is paramount to establishing trust and securing her willingness to participate.

You must respect each woman's independence and decisions. The goal of the leaders is to provide a safe, supportive environment for women to share, grow, and transform. Spiritual transformation occurs by (a) learning the truth of the Word of God, (b) integrating and practicing what is learned, (c) reflecting on the success/failure of what new attitudes and behaviors were attempted, and (d) sharing each other's experiences within the supportive group, thus allowing them to progress on their journey of healing and wholeness in Christ.[159]

> CONNECTING WITH EACH VICTIM IS PARAMOUNT TO ESTABLISHING TRUST AND SECURING HER WILLINGNESS TO PARTICIPATE.

And Christ gave gifts to people—he made some to be apostles, some to be prophets, some to go and tell the Good News, and some to have the work of caring for and teaching God's people. Christ gave those gifts to prepare God's holy people for the work of serving, to make the body of Christ stronger. This work must

continue until we are all joined together in the same faith and in the same knowledge of the Son of God. We must become like a mature person, growing until we become like Christ and have his perfection.
Ephesians 4:11-13 NCV

Small Group Sessions

When starting a new group, it is essential to provide opportunities for informal conversation to allow personal contact between group members. This can be as informal as pre-group snacks or as formal as planned ice-breakers. Each woman needs to feel comfortable with her fellow participants before she will share her story.

Each meeting time should have a specific lesson to be covered. However, as noted previously, it is important to allow the time to be directed by the Holy Spirit. If a woman is obviously in distress, it is important to ask if she wants to share with the group or talk privately to a leader. A guideline for how a group would progress is below:

- Allow a short time of fellowship.
- Open each meeting with prayer.
- Ask for a quick review of the last topic. [Helps those who missed the previous week.]
- Share the lesson focus for this session.
- Ask for previous knowledge about the topic.
- Present the lesson through both written materials and discussion, if possible. Facilitate interaction. A culminating reflective activity is a great way to end the lesson. It can be as simple telling one thing learned, journaling, (if keeping a journal is safe), having each woman write on a sticky note one Scripture from the lesson that really spoke to her, or sketching a picture of something that impacted her to take with her. The lesson should include:
  - an explanation of the concept being covered with accompanying Scriptures

  - Biblical and other examples that illustrate the concept
  - guidance on how the concept can be applied to our own lives

- Ask the women to share how the lesson applies to them.

- Complete the lesson with a recap of what was learned.

- Close with a time of worship and/or prayer.

Encouraging Group Participation

The desire of any small group is that each person actively partic-ipates. To facilitate maximum group interaction, you can learn how best to make each woman feel safe and comfortable by periodically asking the group a few gentle questions. Let the group know you will be writing down their answers to help you remember everyone's wishes.

- *How would you describe your most comfortable place? What about it brings you comfort?* It may be something as easy to accommo-date as a room with low lighting, making sure there are windows in the room, or arranging seating so she doesn't sit with her back to the door.

- *What makes it easier to share your experiences?* It may be allowing others to go first, going first herself, walking around while talking, or writing things down first then reading to the group, coloring or doodling .

- *What makes it harder for you to share?* Making eye contact or be-ing asked to speak louder may hinder her participation.

- *What kinds of things can the group do to support you as you share?* Examples of answers might be affirming by nodding of heads, qui-etly listening, looking at the speaker, repeating back what was said.

- *What kinds of things would you prefer the group avoid doing while you are sharing?* Typical answers would be interrupting, giving advice, side conversations, texting, playing on a cell phone, telling her what she should have done, or not paying attention.

- *How do you best learn: if you read something yourself, if you listen while someone else talks about/reads something, if you write down something, and/or if you do activities to help you remember something?* Design your lessons to meet all of these learning styles.

Keys to Leading a Discussion

I have yet to meet a victim who is not in or has not experienced emotional and/or physical pain. She has a tremendous need to be heard and validated. She may have been silenced for years, her opinions and emotions dismissed. As a result, sharing the traumatic events of her abusive relationship is part of the healing process and may take time. Each woman deserves whatever amount of time it takes for her to be comfortable enough to share parts or all of her story. She may have hindrances to communicating.

- She may have difficulty sharing thoughts and feelings.

- She may be extremely sensitive to perceived criticism.

- She may experience "triggers" during the lesson. A trigger is something that sets off a flashback or remembrance of a traumatic event. Sights, sounds, smells, movements, other sensory input, and situations can spark triggers.[160] Triggers are individual, very personal, and have a real source with real emotions attached: distress, fear, helplessness, guilt, shame, anxiety, depression, or anger.[161]

"The real issue in listening isn't whether we do or don't give advice but whether or not our response is focused on reading and responding to the other person's feelings or is simply a way of dealing with our own."[162]

Many factors are important when having a conversation with the group: proximity, body language, word choice, volume, tone, eye contact, active listening, and validation. (See Resource 10) Many times, until the emotions are recognized and acknowledged, little to no processing of information can occur. "The more emotional our experience, the less we can think clearly, resist impulses, and engage in constructive problem-solving. Only after calm is restored can we begin to address the issue with the rational part of the brain."[163]

When victims have been silenced for years, we offer them a precious gift in the knowledge that they are believed, validated, understood, supported, and not alone. What a tremendous ministry of God!

WHEN VICTIMS HAVE BEEN SILENCED FOR YEARS, WE OFFER THEM A PRECIOUS GIFT IN THE KNOWLEDGE THAT THEY ARE BELIEVED, VALIDATED, UNDERSTOOD, SUPPORTED, AND NOT ALONE. WHAT A TREMENDOUS MINISTRY OF GOD!

Self-Care for Group Leaders

The ministry to victims of domestic violence can be emotionally draining. We must take responsibility for keeping ourselves spiritually, physically, and mentally healthy. It is important that all those involved in direct interaction with victims recognize their susceptibility to burnout and vicarious trauma. Beware of decreased productivity, nightmares, feelings of hopelessness, guilt, incompetence, paranoia, PTSD, and withdrawing from family and friends.[164]

"It can be a windy and treacherous path for those caring enough to stick it out alongside an abused woman. They can experience the highs and lows of the abusive relationship as if they are the ones being abused."[165] Below is a list of ways you can be proactive in avoiding negative by-products of this ministry.

- Know the signs that indicate you and/or others are reaching your limit.

- Know your own personal triggers.

- Let other leaders know if you need to talk about your feelings.

- Expand your base of training and support by meeting with others involved in this ministry. Swap coping skills.

- Understand you can't help everyone. Remember the ones you did help.

- Keep balance in your life. This ministry is only one part of it.

- Step away as often as you need.

- Exercise.

- Use your creative talents.

- Keep your eyes focused on Jesus.[166]

Let us consider how to inspire each other to greater love and to righteous deeds, not forgetting to gather as a community, as some have forgotten, but encouraging each other, especially as the day of His return approaches. Hebrews 10:24-25 Voice

Declaration

"The enemy wanted to change your destiny through a series of events, but God will restore you to wholeness as if the events had never happened. The triumphant woman locked inside shall come forth to where she belongs. He's delivering her. He's releasing her. He's restoring her. He's building her back. He's bringing her out. He's delivering her by the power of His Spirit. *'Not by might, not by power, but by My Spirit, saith the Lord of hosts'* (Zech. 6:6)"[167]

Chapter 15

The Perils of Couple or Marital Counseling in Cases of Abuse

For they do not speak peace, but they devise
deceitful words [half-truths and lies] against those
who are quiet in the land. Psalm 35:20 AMP

There are many times when victims dealing with domestic abuse will be advised to seek counseling, see a therapist, or seek advice from a professional. This suggestion is the opposite of what agencies and organizations dedicated to helping victims of abuse and holding abusers accountable recommend. These organizations caution against any type of relationship counseling until the abuser has successfully completed a Batterer Intervention Program and demonstrates a genuine change in behavior and attitudes. Unfortunately, many professionals, clergy, and Christian counselors to whom a victim might disclose abuse have not been made aware of the perils of relationship counseling for victims.[168] Violent behavior must be addressed and stopped before couples counseling takes place. Treating couples together before the violence is stopped could:

1. Endanger the battered woman who may face violence or threats of violence for revealing information during therapy which is disapproved by her partner;

2. Lend credence to the common misunderstanding that battered women are responsible for the violence inflicted upon them;

3. Ignore the denial, minimization, and deception about the violence that occurs when the focus of counseling is on the couple's interaction;

4. Indicate that the therapist condones violence or that violence is acceptable or not important;

5. Reinforce stereotypic sex roles, thereby ignoring the battered woman's right and responsibility to choose whether or not to save the relationship;

6. Increase the battered woman's sense of isolation, as she may prevaricate about the violence because she is afraid to speak up, even in therapy. This can have the effect of discouraging her from taking any other positive action to eliminate the violence inflicted upon her;

7. Imply that the battered woman has responsibility for seeing that the batterer gets help. Therapists need to be particularly wary of the manipulation inherent in a batterer's refusal of anything other than couple treatment.[169]

Additionally, the counselor may be hesitant to confront just one partner to avoid the appearance of favoritism. Other victims may have a false sense of security and safety to disclose the abuse believing the therapist will keep her safe, resulting in retaliatory abuse after leaving. Some victims may feel obligated to stay longer in an abusive situation than if she were not in counseling due to the time commitment requirement, usually a minimum of several weeks, of some counselors.[170]

Victim: After I had gone back home again after leaving, we went to a professional counselor for three sessions. I was already tense because we *were riding together. The first session was spent with both of us taking an assessment. In the second session we actually met with the counselor. The first problem came when the topic of sex came up, and the counselor agreed with my husband that "sometimes men just want to f***." He said those exact words. My stomach knotted because he had just given my husband permission to take sex. The second problem was when I tried to explain how afraid I was all the time and my husband stormed out. He wasn't going to sit there and "listen to my bullsh*t." The counselor treated it as if it were perfectly okay for my husband to storm out. He never addressed the cause of my fear but asked what I did when I was afraid. I told him, "Pray." I then received a condescending speech about how some people used religion as a crutch, but in my case, he could see I really seemed to think it helped. He made me feel more powerless than I already did. Did I mention that when I got to the car that day my husband was furious? I paid for that comment about being afraid of him for days. He made sure I wouldn't say it again. There were no more couples counseling sessions after that, even though he had promised he would go if I came back home. I did go back to the counselor by myself for another session, but honestly, I felt worse off than better.*

The problem in abusive homes cannot be addressed in couples counseling or marriage counseling because the problem is not with the couple or the marriage. The problem lies solely with the abuser and the answer lies solely with the abuser. Unless there is an awareness of domestic violence dynamics and knowledge that there is abuse in the couple's home, the professional may unwittingly increase the danger to the victim and increase her sense of hopelessness. Counselors may assume the victim has the freedom to talk about the violence. Even professionals who are aware of the risk to the victim plow ahead with the counseling in individual sessions or together as a couple, choosing to treat the problems as relational instead of devastating criminal behavior.

"Unfortunately, many ministers graduating from Bible college, university, or seminary may have had only one or two courses in

Christian counseling."[171] And yet, "70 percent of Protestant pastors reported using marriage or couples counseling when dealing with domestic and sexual violence situations."[172]

Listed below are ways an abuser can and will maliciously and deliberately manipulate and derail relationship counseling, re-victimizing his partner.

1. The abuser will magnanimously accompany his partner to the sessions as a gesture of his goodwill and generosity. Since he doesn't believe there is a problem with him in the relationship, he has nothing to worry about.

2. The counselor will focus on validating his positive behaviors such as his continued attendance and his support for his partner. He has no intention of examining his behavior and attitudes or making any changes. His partner, who is genuinely seeking help and change, is willing to look closely at her behavior and make the necessary changes for the sake of the relationship.

3. He may look forward to pointing out the flaws in his partner and gaining an ally in the counselor who will focus attention on the personality flaws, faults, bad habits, and weaknesses of the victim.

4. To create credibility and control, the abuser may appear to be cooperative as long as the discussions are following the path he desires. He may succeed in convincing the counselor he is the true victim of abuse or that he is the healthy one in the relationship.

5. He will spin his partner's version of events around to his advantage by contradicting or denying them. The impartial, nonjudgmental counselor listens with an open mind while the victim listens helplessly to his manipulative lies and excuses/justifications, afraid of losing the counselor's help or risking the abuser's retaliation if she speaks up.

6. If he does reluctantly agree to talk about his beliefs and behaviors, he may be encouraged by the counselor to safely vent his anger and express his feelings that "cause" him to abuse his partner. The counselor has just become his approving audience as he spews forth all his justifications about why his partner angers him and provokes him to violence while never touching on his domination and control behaviors. His victim is justifiably dismayed.

7. He may insist on driving her to her individual counseling appointments and remain nearby, hindering her from confiding in the counselor. He may interrogate her about what was said or punish her if she refuses to reveal the conversations.

8. He may give his partner false or misquoted reports about her that the counselor has supposedly confided to him, under the guise of making sure she is fully aware of what the counselor believes. He may tell her the counselor thinks she has a serious personality disorder or mental illness. He may insinuate that the counselor thinks she is the one with the problem, and the one mistreating him.

9. If his partner does ask the counselor if the statements are true, and he is confronted by the counselor for giving wrong information, he will deny saying them, making his partner appear manipulative or delusional.[173]

*Be sober-minded; be watchful. Your adversary
the devil prowls around like a roaring lion, seeking
someone to devour. I Peter 5:8 ESV*

The abuser rarely will have his lies, deceptions, and manipulations confronted because traditional counseling methods are focused on validating and focusing on the positive, while gently correcting.

The following are ways a counselor can cause more harm and re-victimize the victim:

1. The victim may be advised to ignore the negative behavior and praise him when he is not being abusive. Essentially, she is being asked to praise him for not beating her or not calling her a slut.

2. The victim may be told to try to see things from his point of view, giving the impression of validating his controlling attitudes and behavior. His point of view is that he owns his partner and is entitled to treat her however he wishes. How does that help the victim?

3. The abuser may be given carte blanche to continue his abuse. It is unconscionable for a counselor to state in the presence of the abuser, "Everyone is entitled to live according to his own beliefs and opinions." *His beliefs are the root of his abusive behavior!* In addition, the counselor has inadvertently given the abuser more ammunition to use against his partner in the future. What an injustice to the victim!

4. Counselors may tell the victim just to ignore the abuse, as if it will go away. It is *never* acceptable to purposefully ignore or excuse abuse. While urging the victim to show more respect and under-standing for her partner by pretending the abuse is not happen-ing, the counselor has not only failed to confront the abuser on the victim's behalf but has given him unspoken encouragement to increase his power tactics. It is ridiculous to show respect for disrespectful, deceitful, domineering attitudes and actions.

5. Counselors may treat abuse as if it were simply bad manners. By modeling "nice manners," they expect to change an abuser's attitudes and behaviors. This is beyond naive. Abusers are aware of social conventions and choose whom to respect according to their own advantage. They choose not to respect their partners, preferring to dominate and oppress them instead.

6. The victim may be asked to compromise. Urging a victim to "be more understanding" and "meet him halfway" will result in him using it for manipulation and control. He will align himself with the counselor and pressure his partner to meet him halfway, even when he makes degrading, excessive, or unfair demands. The pressure to compromise encourages her to override her own intuition and common sense. A woman who has been raped by her partner could be urged to resume some physical displays of affection as a sign of her support and encouragement for him and prevent greater difficulty reconciling. The abuser's entitlement attitude toward his partner's body is never addressed nor is his aggressive approach to sex.

Victim: Every counseling session was a nightmare. We fought worse in the parking lot after each session than all the week leading up to it. Anything I addressed was thrown back in my face. And our Christian counselor was a woman. It felt like a slap in the face that she couldn't see how I was being abused both verbally and sexually. During one session, I brought up when my husband threatened to throw a toaster into the bathtub with my 2- and 3-year-old nephews. Her response was that I needed to leave those things in the past. In another session, we focused on our intimate relationship. I told her I just didn't feel comfortable having sex, that I had no drive, and I didn't want to do it. He wanted to do it every day. Her compromise was that we do it three times a week. We fought in the parking lot in our car for an hour that night. He felt he had gotten the worse end of the deal. I felt like I had been condemned to being raped three times a week.

7. Counselors can also urge a victim to compromise her defined boundaries. Setting and enforcing boundaries is already difficult for victims. Asking her to compromise and allow her boundaries to be crossed puts her at greater risk for further abuse. The abuser may offer apologies and promises yet still has demonstrated no change in his core beliefs and attitudes. All of the compro-

mising is on the part of the victim who has every reason *not* to compromise.

8. Poor word choice by counselors when countering abusive statements and patterns of behavior can send the wrong message. By telling abusers they need to "allow" their partner more autonomy, financial control, or participate in any other activity implies the right of the abuser to control his partner. One partner "allowing" the other to do anything speaks more of a parent-child relationship rather than a partnership of adults.[174]

Individual Counseling

A victim seeking counseling without her partner can often be at risk of the counselor's inaccurate assessment. She may present as a mental and emotional wreck. The counselor has no idea of the victim's state of mind prior to the abuse. By the time the victim gets to the counselor, there may be multiple concerns with her emotional health. The cause and effect of abuse may never be considered. Counselors may be unsure which came first, the psychological issues or the abuse. The reality of the abuse may be seen as a bent toward feeling persecuted, a distortion of reality, or a misrepresentation of the facts. Her motives for sharing her story may be questioned. She may be told she has a victim mentality or is delusional. The counselor's mistaken assumptions about the victim can lead to an examination of her emotional, relational, and familial history, totally missing the mark. The abuser wins again without even being there. His partner is questioning her own sanity and mental health, something he may have already expressed to her and others.[175]

Victim: We had only been married a few weeks when the first major incident occurred. I realized I had made a terrible mistake but was too embarrassed to tell anybody. My mom had tried to warn me not to marry him. I finally realized I needed to talk to somebody, so I started going to a counselor at a local church. I didn't know how to explain to him what was going on except I was afraid when my husband drank and acted mean. The counselor wanted to know all about my childhood, my relationship with my father, and my night dreams. My fear and sense of hopelessness grew as nothing was changing at home except my husband was now saying I didn't need to talk to a shrink – I could talk to him. Finally, I didn't know what else to do. I tried to kill myself. I would have succeeded except for the grace of God. I did tell my counselor about my suicide attempt; he was very surprised. He had no idea I was so desperate. I guess I was good even back then at pretending everything was okay. I stopped seeing the counselor after that.

Lundy Bancroft states change in abusers comes only when they let go of the idea that their partner has any role in causing their abuse of her.[176] They have to stop focusing on their feelings and her behavior and start focusing on her feelings and their behavior. He further advises waiting until the abuse has been completely absent from the relationship for two years before ever seeing a couples counselor.

SPECIALIZED PROGRAMS FOR ABUSERS ARE VERY DIFFERENT FROM THERAPY.

Specialized programs for abusers are very different from therapy. They educate abusers about abuse and confront their attitudes and excuses. Therapy focuses on the abuser's feelings; abuser programs focus on his thinking. Therapy usually does not focus on the core causal issues of abuse (entitlement, disrespect, selfishness, projecting blame, desire for control); abuser programs focus on each cause.[177]

Unfortunately, the majority of abusers choose not to do the hard work required to change. It's not that they can't change, but they decide they don't want to.[178] The ones who make the greatest changes for the longest periods are those whose family and friends call him out on his abuse and support the victim instead of him; who show empathy early on about the pain he has caused his partner; whose victim receives absolute support from family, friends, the faith community, and the legal system; and who successfully completes a quality extended abuser program for about two years.[179] He will get serious about changing when the discomfort of staying the same becomes greater than the discomfort of changing.[180]

For a good tree does not bear bad fruit, nor does a bad tree bear good fruit. For every tree is known by its own fruit. For men do not gather figs from thorns, nor do they gather grapes from a bramble bush. A good man out of the good treasure of his heart brings forth good; and an evil man out of the evil treasure of his heart brings forth evil. For out of the abundance of the heart his mouth speaks.
Luke 6:43-45 NKJV

A Final Note

Many prayers have been spoken during the years it has taken for this project to become a reality. To all of you who read this book, I offer my sincerest appreciation. I pray God will raise up those in your area who are and will be called to this ministry. My heart swells with joy as I picture the body of Christ becoming a beacon of help and hope for all those affected by violence in the home.

I seriously doubt all those years ago my advocates would have thought the terrified, sobbing mess of a woman in front of them would one day write a book to help others as they helped me. We don't always get to see the fruit of our labors, but please know every listening ear, every kind act, every spark of hope makes a difference.

> EVERY LISTENING EAR, EVERY KIND ACT, EVERY SPARK OF HOPE MAKES A DIFFERENCE.

Whether you are a survivor, an advocate, a friend or family member of a victim, or a church leader, I hope you truly grasp the magnitude of this ministry. You are helping women break free of the destruction and devastation resulting from domestic violence. Through the power of God working through you, you are helping victims become survivors and thrivers. You are not just being used by God to help a single person or a single family. You are being used by God to change generations upon generations.

I pray blessings over you all.

You are the light of the world. A city set on a hill cannot be hidden. Nor do people light a lamp and put it under a basket, but on a stand, and it gives light to all in the house.

In the same way, let your light shine before others, so that they may see your good works and give glory to your Father who is in heaven. Matthew 5:14-16 ESV

Endnotes

1 Black, M.C., Basile, K.C., Breiding, M.J., ietnanith, S.G., Walters, M.L., Merrick, M.T., Chen, J. & Stevens, M. (2011). *The National Intimate Partner and Sexual Violence Survey: 2010 Summary Report.* Retrieved from http://www.cdc.gov/violenceprevention/pdf/nisvs_report2010-a.pdf.

2 National Center for Injury Prevention and Control, Centers for Disease Control and Prevention (n.d.). *Infographic Based on Data from the National Intimate Partner and Sexual Violence Survey (NISVS): 2010-2012 State Report.* https://www.cdc.gov/violenceprevention/pdf/ NISVS-infographic-2016.pdf.

3 Black, M.C., Basile, K.C., Breiding, M.J., Smith, S.G., Walters, M.L., Merrick, M.T., Chen, J. & Stevens, M. *The National Intimate Partner and Sexual Violence Survey: 2010 Summary Report.*

4 Ibid.

5 Ibid.

6 Ibid.

7 National Network to End Domestic Violence (2017). *Domestic Violence Counts National Summary.* Retrieved from https://nnedv.org/ mdocs- posts/census_2016_handout_national-summary/.

8 Campbell, J.C., Webster, D., Koziol-McLain, J., Block, C., Campbell, D., Curry, M. A., Gary, F., Glass, N., McFarlane, J., Sachs, C., Sharps, P., Ulrich, Y., Wilt, S., Manganello, J., Xu, X., Schollenberger, J., Frye, V. & Lauphon, K. (2003). Risk factors for femicide in abusive relationships: Results from a multisite case control study. *American Journal of Public Health*, 93(7), 1089-1097.

9 Truman, J. L. & Morgan, R. E. (2014). *Nonfatal Domestic Violence, 2003-2012.* Retrieved from http://www.bjs.gov/content/pub/pdf/ ndv0312.pdf.

10 Ibid.

11 Ibid.

12-15 Material omitted.

16 Bridges, F.S., Tatum, K. M., & Kunselman, J.C. (2008). Domestic violence statutes and rates of intimate partner and family homicide: A research note. *Criminal Justice Policy Review,* 19(1), 117-130.

17 Smith, S., Fowler, K. & Niolon, P. (2014). Intimate partner homicide and corollary victims in 16 states: National violent death reporting system, 2003-2009. *American Journal of Public Health,* 104(3), 461-466. doi: 10.2105/AJPH.2013.301582.

18 Violence Policy Center. (2012). *American Roulette: Murder-Suicide in the United States.* Retrieved from www.vpc.org/studies/amroul2012.pdf.

19 Ibid.

20 World Health Organization (2013). *Global and regional estimates of violence against women: Prevalence and health effects of intimate partner violence and non-partner sexual violence.* Retrieved from http://apps.who.int/iris/bitstream/10665/85239/1/9789241564625_eng.pdf?ua=1.

21 Ibid.

22 Truman, J. L. & Morgan, R. E. (2014). *Nonfatal Domestic Violence, 2003-2012.* Retrieved from http://www.bjs.gov/content/pub/pdf/ndv0312.pdf.

23 Rothman, E., Hathaway, J., Stidsen, A. & de Vries, H. (2007). How employment helps female victims of intimate partner abuse: A qualitative study. *Journal of Occupational Health Psychology,* 12(2), 136-143. doi: 10.1037/1076-8998.12.2.136.

24 World Health Organization (2004). *The Economic Dimensions of Interpersonal Violence.* Retrieved from http://apps.who.int/iris/bitstream/10665/42944/1/9241591609.pdf.

25 Ibid.

26 Finkelhor, D., Turner, H., Ormrod, R. & Hamby, S. (2011). *Children's Exposure to Intimate Partner Violence and Other Family Violence.* Retrieved from https://www.ncjrs.gov/pdffiles1/ojjdp/232272.pdf.

27 Black, M.C., Basile, K.C., Breiding, M.J., Smith, S.G., Walters, M.L., Merrick, M.T., Chen, J. & Stevens, M. (2011). *The National Intimate Partner and Sexual Violence Survey: 2010 Summary Report.* Retrieved from http://www.cdc.gov/violenceprevention/pdf/nisvs_report2010-a.pdf.

28 LifeWay Research: Biblical Solutions for Life (2004). *Pastors and Domestic and Sexual Violence: Survey of 1,000 Protestant Pastors.* https://lifewayresearch.com/2014/06/27/ pastors-seldom-preach-about-domestic-violence/.

29 United Nations Office on Drugs and Crime (2018). *Global Study on Homicide: Gender-related Killing of Women and Girls.* https://www. unodc.org/documents/data-and-analysis/GSH2018/GSH18_Gender-related_killing_of_women_and_girls.pdf.

30 Caringchurches.com. (2003). "What Churches Can Do to Address Domestic Violence" interview with Lynette Hoy. https://www.crosswalk. com/family/marriage/what-churches-can-do-to-address-domestic-abuse-11596483.html.

31 LifeWay Research: Biblical Solutions for Life (2004) *Pastors and Domestic and Sexual Violence: Survey of 1,000 Protestant Pastors.* https://lifewayresearch.com/2014/06/27/ pastors-seldom-preach-about-domestic-violence/.

32 United Nations Entity for Gender Equality and the Empowerment of Women Virtual Knowledge Center to End Violence Against Women and Girls (2012). "Safety Assessment and Planning". http://www.end-vawnow.org/en/articles/669-safety-assessment-and-planning.html.

33 Bancroft, Lundy. *Why Does He Do That? Inside the Minds of Angry and Controlling Men.* (New York, NY: Berkley Books, 2002). 339-342.

34 FaithTrust Institute (2014). "What Faith Community Can Do to Respond to Domestic Violence". https://www.faithtrustinstitute.org/ resources/articles/What-Faith-Community-Can-Do%202014.pdf.

35 Kroeger, Catherine Clark, and Nancy Nason-Clark. *No Place for Abuse: Biblical and Practical Resources to Counteract Domestic Violence.* (Downers Grove, IL: InterVarsity Press, 2010), 16-17.

36 Meurer FSM, Jeanne (2008) Speaker, "Faith Communities Uniting to End Domestic Violence." St. Charles, MO.

37 Alpert, Elaine J. *Responding to Domestic Violence: An Interfaith Guide to Prevention and Intervention.* The Chicago Metropolitan Battered Women's Network, (2005). Retrieved August 3, 2009. https://www.familyministries.org/files/1.1.1.%20Responding%20to%20Domestic%20Violence%20An%20Interfaith%20Guide.pdf. 9-12.

38 Women Against Abuse website: http://www.womenagainstabuse.org/education-resources/learn-about-abuse/what-is-domestic-violence.

39 The Council on Biblical Manhood and Womanhood website: https://cbmw.org/about/statement-on-abuse/.

40 Leaf, Dr. Caroline. *The Gift in You.* (US: In, Ltd., 2009). 146-147.

41 Adapted from "8 Steps That Explain 'Why She Doesn't Leave,'" *Huffington Post* website: https://www.huffingtonpost.com/crystal-sanchez/8-steps-that-explain-why-_b_9143360.html.

42 Mohammed, Mildred D. "Silent Scars of Domestic Abuse" (2018) from The National Domestic Violence Hotline Website: https://www.thehotline.org/2018/08/25/silent-scars-of-domestic-abuse/.

43 "What is Psychological Abuse?" from the National Coalition Against Domestic Violence website: https://www.speakcdn.com/assets/2497/domestic_violence_and_psychological_abuse_ncadv.pdf.

44 "Types of Verbal Abuse" from Abigail's website: http://www.abigails.org/Sin/types-of-verbal-abuse.htm.

45 "Facts About Domestic Violence and Economic Abuse" from National Coalition Against Domestic Violence website: https://www.speakcdn.com/assets/2497/domestic_violence_and_economic_abuse_ncadv.pdf.

46 "Financial Abuse Hidden Within Christianity" from Ashley Easter website: http://www.ashleyeaster.com/blog/financial-abuse.

47 "Facts About Domestic Violence and Economic Abuse" from National Coalition Against Domestic Violence website: https://www.speakcdn.com/assets/2497/domestic_violence_and_economic_abuse_ncadv.pdf.

48 "Types of Abuse" from Arizona Coalition to End Sexual and Domestic Violence website: https://www.acesdv.org/domestic-violence-graphics/types-of-abuse/.

49 "What is Intimate Partner Physical Abuse?" from the National Coalition Against Domestic Violence website: https://www.speakcdn.com/assets/2497/domestic_violence_and_physical_abuse_ncadv.pdf.

50 Brewster, Susan M.S.S.W. *Helping Her Get Free: A Guide for Families and Friends of Abused Women* (Emeryville, CA: Seal Press, 2006). 8-9.

51 "Understanding the Nature and Dynamics of Sexual Violence." Missouri Coalition Against Domestic and Sexual Violence. 1-2.

52 "Domestic and Sexual Assault" from National Coalition Against Domestic Violence website: https://www.speakcdn.com/assets/2497/sexual_assault_dv.pdf.

53 Ibid.

54 Bancroft, *Why Does He Do That?* 174-185.

55 Klein, Andrew R. (2009) *Practical Implications of Current Domestic Violence Research: For Law Enforcement, Prosecutors, and Judges.* U.S. Department of Justice National Institute of Justice Special Report. 2-3. From the U.S. Department of Justice website: https://www.ncjrs.gov/pdffiles1/nij/225722.pdf.

56 "Domestic and Sexual Assault" from National Coalition Against Domestic Violence website: https://www.speakcdn.com/assets/2497/sexual_assault_dv.pdf.

57 Domestic Violence Statistics website: https://domesticviolencestatistics.org/domestic-violence-statistics/.

58 Brewster, *Helping Her Get Free,* 50.

59 National Coalition Against Domestic Violence. "Who is Doing What to Whom? Determining the Core Aggressor in Relationships Where Domestic Violence Exists" from their website: https://www.speakcdn.com/assets/2497/who_is_doing_what_to_whom.pdf.

60 Murphy, Clare Ph.D. "Language Women Should Use in Family Court." SpeakOutLoud.net. website: https://speakoutloud.net/institutional-abuse/child-custody/language-of-resistance-in-family-court.

61 Bancroft, *Why Does He Do That?* x.

62 The Missouri Coalition Against Domestic and Sexual Violence. *Understanding the Nature and Dynamics of Domestic Violence* (revised 2014), 1.

63 The National Domestic Violence Hotline. "Supporting Someone Who Keeps Returning to an Abusive Relationship" (2017) from their website: https://www.thehotline.org/2017/02/16/supporting-someone-returning-to-abusive-relationship/.

64 Zoellner, L. A., Feeny, N.C., Alvarez, J., Watlington, C., O'Neill, M. L., Zager, R. et al. (2000). "Factors Associated with Completion of the Restraining Order Process in Female Victims of Partner Violence." *Journal of Interpersonal Violence,* 15(10), 1081–1099.

65 Laws.com. "Beware of Domestic Violence Repeat Offenders" from their website: https://marriage.laws.com/domestic-violence/domestic-violence-statistics/repeat-offenders.

66 Arizona Coalition Against Domestic Violence (2000). *Best Practices Manual for Domestic Violence Programs.* 25-26. From the ncdsv.org website: http://www.ncdsv.org/images/Best%20Practices%20Manual%20for%20DV%20Prgrms_AZCADV.pdf.

67 "Intimate Partner Violence: Consequences" from Center for Disease Control website: https://www.cdc.gov/violenceprevention/intimatepartnerviolence/consequences.html.

68 Ibid.

69 Ibid.

70 "Domestic Violence and Child Abuse" from Children's Hospital of Philadelphia Research Institute website: https://injury.research.chop.edu/violence-prevention-initiative/types-violence-involving-youth/domestic-violence-and-child-abuse#.XFufBi2ZPy9.

71 "Statistics" from National Coalition Against Domestic Violence website: https://ncadv.org/statistics.

72 "The Facts on Children and Domestic Violence" from Futures Without Violence website: https://www.futureswithoutviolence.org/userfiles/file/Children_and_Families/Children.pdf.

73 Ibid.

74 Ibid.

75 "Domestic Violence and Child Abuse" from Children's Hospital of Philadelphia Research Institute website: https://injury.research.chop.edu/violence-prevention-initiative/types-violence-involving-youth/domestic-violence-and-child-abuse#.XFumSy2ZPy9.

76 Ibid.

77 Ibid.

78 Ibid.

79 Ibid.

80 October 2016 Domestic Violence Fact Sheet from National Council of Juvenile and Family Court Judges website: https://www.ncjfcj.org/sites/default/files/NCJFCJ_DVAM_FactSheet_2016_Final_1.pdf.

81 Resource Center on Domestic Violence: Child Protection and Custody website: https://rcdvcpc.org/facts.html.

82 Ibid.

83 "Domestic Violence and Child Abuse" from Children's Hospital of Philadelphia Research Institute website: https://injury.research.chop.edu/violence-prevention-initiative/types-violence-involving-youth/domestic-violence-and-child-abuse#.XFuF-S2ZMmI.

84 Bancroft, Lundy. *When Dad Hurts Mom: Helping Your Children Heal the Wounds of Witnessing Abuse.* (New York, NY: Berkley Books 2004). 314-315.

85 Ibid.

86 Bancroft, *Why Does He Do That?* 42-75.

87 Bancroft, *When Dad Hurts Mom*, 313.

88 Ibid, 78-101.

89 Bancroft, *Why Does He Do That?* viii-vix.

90 Ibid, 34-35.

91 Ibid, 14-48.

92 Herman, K., Rotunda, R., Williamson, G., & Vodanovich, S. (2014). "Outcomes from a Duluth Model Batterer Intervention Program at Completion and Long Term Follow- up." *Journal of Offender Rehabilitation,* 53(1), 1-18.

93 Piper, John. "Clarifying Words on Wife Abuse" (2012) © Desiring God Foundation from Desiring God website: https://www.desiringgod.org/articles/clarifying-words-on-wife-abuse.

94 The Missouri Coalition Against Domestic and Sexual Violence. *Understanding the Nature and Dynamics of Domestic Violence* (revised 2014), 13.

95 Kroeger and Nason-Clark, *No Place for Abuse*, 62.

96 Sudbury-Wyland-Lincoln Domestic Violence Roundtable. "The Cycle of Domestic Violence," at their website: http://www.domesticvio-lenceroundtable.org/domestic-violence-cycle.html.

97 White Ribbon Australia. "Cycle of Violence," at their website: https://www.whiteribbon.org.au/understand-domestic-violence/what-is-domestic-violence/cycle-of-violence/.

98 Community Beyond Violence. "Cycle of Violence," at their website: htpp://cbv.org/cycles-of-violence/.

99 Ibid.

100 Ibid.

101 Conversation with victims of domestic violence as reported to the author.

102 The National Domestic Violence Hotline. "Is Change Possible In An Abuser?" from their website: https://www.thehotline.org/2013/09/05/is-change-possible-in-an-abuser/.

103 Bancroft, *Why Does He Do That?* 340-342.

104 Hunt, June. *Domestic Violence: Assault on a Woman's Worth* (Peabody, MA: Aspire Press, 2013), 30.

105 Bancroft, *Why Does He Do That?* 276.

106 Bender, Rebecca. *Roadmap to Redemption* (self-published, 2013), 28-33.

107 The Missouri Coalition Against Domestic and Sexual Violence. *Understanding the Nature and Dynamics of Domestic Violence* (revised 2014), 27.

108 National Coalition Against Domestic Violence. 'What Is Domestic Violence?" at their website: https://ncadv.org/learn-more.

109 National Coalition Against Domestic Violence. "Why Do Victims Stay?" at their website https://ncadv.org/why-do-victims-stay.

110 The Missouri Coalition Against Domestic and Sexual Violence. *Understanding the Nature and Dynamics of Domestic Violence* (revised 2014), 8.

111 LaViolette, Alyce D. and Ola W. Barnett. *It Could Happen to Anyone: Why Battered Women Stay.* (Thousand Oaks, CA: Sage Productions, Inc., 2000), 166.

112 Graham, Billy. *Answers to Life's Problems: Guidance, Inspiration and Hope for the Challenges of Today.* (Dallas, TX: Word Publishing, 1988), 37.

113 Kroger and Nason-Clark, *No Place for Abuse*, 181.

114 Ibid, 184-185.

115 Brewster, *Helping Her get Free*, 86-87.

116 Ibid.

117 LaViolette and Barnett, *It Could Happen to Anyone,* 166.

118 Ibid, 145.

119 Kroeger, Catherine Clark. "The Pastor and Domestic Violence," Catalyst, (February 2004), at their website: https://www.catalystresources.org/safeguarding-the-lives-of-the-sheep/.

120 Smietana, Bob. September 18, 2018. "Pastors Seldom Preach About Domestic Violence," LifeWay Research, at their website: https://lifewayresearch.com/2014/06/27/pastors-seldom-preach-about-domestic-violence/.

121 Smietana, Bob. June 27, 2014. "Pastors More Likely to Address Domestic Violence, Still Lack Training," LifeWay Research, at their website: https://lifewayresearch.com/2018/09/18/pastors-more-likely-to-address-domestic-violence-still-lack-training/.

122 Smietana, "Pastors Seldom Preach About Domestic Violence."

123 "DV & the Church," Eagles Wings at their website: http://www.eagleswingsglobal.org/dv---the-church.html.

124 Miles, Al. 2007. "What About All the Men?" Christians for Biblical Equality, at their website: http://e-quality.cbeinternational.org.

125 Miles, Al. *Domestic Violence What Every Pastor Needs to Know* (Minneapolis MN: Augsburg Fortress, 2000), 50-69.

126 Smietana, 2018.

127 "Words are Powerful," Center for Hope and Safety at their website: https://hopeandsafety.org/learn-more/words-are-powerful/.

128 Based on the Grief Cycle model first published in *On Death & Dying*, Elisabeth Kübler-Ross, 1969.

129 Kennedy, Judy. 2005. "Confronting Abuse As Sin," Abigail's, from their website: http://www.abigails.org/Sin/abuse-as-sin.htm.

130 The following five items and all Scripture references were adapted from Leslie Vernick. January 22, 2015. "5 Indicators of an Evil and Wicked Heart," Association of Biblical Counselors from their website: https://christiancounseling.com/blog/counseling/five-indicators-of-an-evil-and-wicked-heart-1/.

131 Kennedy, "Confronting Abuse As Sin."

132 "Ask Yourself, 'Am I Hurting My Partner?'" September 3, 2013. National Domestic Violence Hotline at their website: https://www.thehotline.org/2013/09/03/ask-yourself-am-i-hurting-my-partner/.

133 "Abusive Relationships," Alabama Coalition Against Domestic Violence at their website: http://www.acadv.org/warning-signs/are-you-being-abused/.

134 Bancroft, *Why Does He Do That?* 112-113.

135 Adapted from a paper by Fernando Mederos of Common Purpose. "Talking to Men Who Batter Women," Minnesota Coalition for Battered Women.

136 Bancroft, *Why Does He Do That?* 353.

137 Tracy, Steven R., "Clergy Responses to Domestic Violence," *The Academic Journal of CBE International Priscilla Papers 21,* no.2 (Spring 2007) accessed March 29, 2019, https://www.cbeinternational.org/resources/article/priscilla-papers/clergy-responses-domestic-violence.

138 The list of expectations was adapted and expanded from Lundy Bancroft, *Why Does He Do That? Inside the Mind of Angry and Controlling Men,* 339-342.

139 Fortune, Marie M. and James Polling, "Calling to Accountability: The Church's Response to Abusers," in *Violence against Women and Children: A Christian Theological Sourcebook*, ed. Carol J. Adams and Marie Fortune (New York: The Continuum Publishing Company, 1995), 451.

140 Adams, Carol. *Woman Battering* (Philadelphia, PA: Fortress Press, 1994), 92.

141 This list of church responses was adapted and expanded from "Responding to Domestic Violence What the Religious Community Can Do," Faith Trust Institute from their website: https://faithtrust-institute.org/resources/articles/What-Religious-Leaders-Can-Do.pdf/?searchterm=what%20can%20the%20religious%20community%20do.

142 Kroeger and Nason-Clark, *No Place for Abuse*, 173.

143 Gorman, Julie, "Small Groups in the Local Church," in *Introducing Christian Education: Foundations for the Twenty-first Century*, ed. Michael J. Anthony. (Ada MI: Baker Academic, 2001), 176.

144 Brewster, *Helping Her Get Free*, viii.

145 Strong, James LL.D, S.T.D. *The Strongest Strong's Exhaustive Concordance of the Bible*, fully revised and corrected by John R. Kolenberger III and James A. Swanson. (Grand Rapids, MI: Zondervan, 2001), 1537 and 1463.

146 Welch, Donald W. "Counseling Ministry in Church," in *Introducing Christian Education: Foundations for the Twenty-first Century*, ed. Michael J. Anthony. (Ada MI: Baker Academic, 2001), 249.

147 Collins, Jim. *Beyond Positive Thinking: Success & Motivation in the Scriptures.* (Lake Mary, FL: Excel Books, 2010), 5.

148 Gorman, 177.

149 Ibid, 178.

150 Gaffney, James E. "Recovery Ministries," in *Introducing Christian Education: Foundations for the Twenty-first Century*, ed. Michael J. Anthony. (Ada MI: Baker Academic, 2001), 272.

151 Brewster, *Helping Her Get Free*, x.

152 Gorman, 177 and 183.

153 Houston, James. "Family Life Education," in *Introducing Christian Education: Foundations for the Twenty-first Century*, ed. Michael J. Anthony. (Ada MI: Baker Academic, 2001), 198.

154 Leaf, Dr. Caroline. *Who Switched Off Your Brain?:Solving the Mystery of He Said/She Said.* (Inprov, Ltd., 2011), 103.

155 Ibid, 107.

156 "We Are Here," Distributed by National Center on Domestic and Sexual Violence at their website: http://www.ncdsv.org/images/WeAreHere--bwversion.pdf.

157 Gorman, 176-184.

158 Brewster, *Helping Her Get Free*, 6.

159 Taylor, Nick. "Spiritual Formation," in *Introducing Christian Education: Foundations for the Twenty-first Century*, ed. Michael J. Anthony. (Ada MI: Baker Academic, 2001), 97.

160 "Understanding PTSD Flashbacks and Triggers," PTSDUK. org at their website: https://www.ptsduk.org/what-is-ptsd/understanding-ptsd-flashbacks-and-triggers/.

161 "Trauma and You," NCDSV.org at their website: http://ncdsv.org/images/ODVN_Trauma-and-You_May-2013.pdf.

162 Welch, 251.

163 Noll, Douglas. *De-escalate: How to Calm an Angry Person in 90 Seconds or Less.* (New York, NY: Atria Paperback, 2017), 45.

164 "16 Self-care Tips for Advocates," Domestic Shelters.org. (October 23, 2017) at their website: https://www.domesticshelters.org/articles/taking-care-of-you/16-self-care-tips-for-advocates#.Wf4f0rpFxPZ.

165 Brewster, *Helping Her Get Free*, ix.

166 "16 Self-care Tips for Advocates," (2017).

167 Jakes, T. D. *Woman, Thou Art Loosed! Healing the Wounds of the Past.* (Shippensburg, PA: Destiny Image Publishers, Inc., 2012) 81.

168 Moss, Danni. "When Counseling Facilitates Abuse," Because It Matters ~ Freedom From Abuse in Christianity at the website: https://dannimoss.wordpress.com/articles/abuse-in-the-christian-home/victimsurvivor-series/when-counseling-facilitates-abuse/.

169 "A Policy Statement on Domestic Violence Couples Counseling," Faith Trust Institute at their website: https://faithtrustinstitute.org/resources/articles/Policy-Statement-on-DV-Couples-Counseling.pdf?searchterm=couples+counseling.

170 Summary by Chris Huffine of a discussion by the Tri-County Batterer Intervention Provider Network, 1998 from the website: https://www.co.washington.or.us/CommunityCorrections/VictimServices/Services/upload/12-Reasons-Why-Couples-DV.pdf.

171 Welch, 252.

172 Smietana, "Pastors Seldom Preach About Domestic Violence."

173 Moss, "When Counseling Facilitates Abuse."

174 Ibid.

175 Ibid.

176 Bancroft, *Why Does He Do That?* 352.

177 Ibid, 356.

178 Ibid, 357.

179 Ibid, 365.

180 Bancroft, Lundy and Jac Patrissi. *Should I Stay or Should I Go? A Guide to Knowing If Your Relationship Can– and Should– Be Saved.* (New York: Berkley Books, 2011), 139.

References

Adams, Carol J., and Marie M. Fortune. *Violence against Women and Children: a Christian Theological Sourcebook.* Continuum, 1998.

Addison, Doug. *Personal Development God's Way.* Destiny Image Publishers, 2010.

Addison, Doug. *God Spoke, Now What? Activating Your Prophetic Word. InLight Connection,* 2016.

American Bible Society. *The Lord Hears Your Cries.* American Bible Society, 1995.

Anthony, Michael J. *Introducing Christian Education: Foundations for the Twenty-First Century.* Ada MI: Baker Academic, 2001.

Bancroft, Lundy, and Jay G. Silverman. *The Batterer as Parent: Addressing the Impact of Domestic Violence on Family Dynamics.* Sage Publications, 2002.

Bancroft, Lundy, and JAC Patrissi. *Should I Stay or Should I Go? A Guide to Sorting out Whether Your Relationship Can--and Should--Be Saved.* Penguin Group, 2011.

Bancroft, Lundy. *When Dad Hurts Mom: Helping Your Children Heal the Wounds of Witnessing Abuse.* Berkley Publishing Group, 2005.

Bancroft, Lundy. *Why Does He Do That? Inside the Minds of Angry and Controlling Men.* Berkley Books, 2003.

Barnett, Ola, et al. *Family Violence across the Lifespan: An Introduction.* Sage Publications, Inc., 2005.

Bender, Rebecca, and Kathy Bryan. *Elevate: Taking Your Life to the Next Level, a Mentoring Toolkit.* Publisher Unknown, 2017.

Bender, Rebecca. *Roadmap to Redemption: a Faith Based, Comprehensive Workbook Designed to Help Survivors of Sex Trafficking Overcome Their Past and Move Forward toward Their Future.* Publisher Unknown, 2013.

Bowley, Mary Frances. *The White Umbrella: Walking with Survivors of Sex Trafficking.* Moody Publishers, 2012.

Brewster, Susan. *Helping Her Get Free: a Guide for Families and Friends of Abused Women.* Seal Press, 2006.

Cerullo, David. *God's Answers for Your Times of Trouble.* Inspiration Ministries, 2011.

Collins, Jim. *Beyond Positive Thinking: Success and Motivation in the Scriptures.* Excel Books, 2010.

Cummings D.B.S., Chloe. *What Would Jesus Do about Domestic Violence and Abuse Toward Christian Women?* Booklocker.com, Inc., 2011.

DeMoss, Nancy Leigh. *Lies Women Believe.* Moody Publishers, 2001.

DeMoss, Nancy Leigh., and Dannah Gresh. *Lies Young Women Believe.* Moody Publishers, 2008.

Evans, Patricia. *The Verbally Abusive Man--Can He Change? A Woman's Guide to Deciding Whether to Stay or Go.* Adams Media, 2006.

Fortune, Marie M. *Keeping the Faith.* Harper Collins Publishers Inc., 1987.

Fortune, Marie M. *Violence in the Family: A Workshop Curriculum for Clergy and Other Helpers.* Pilgrim Press, 1991.

Gill, A.L., and Joyce Gill. *New Creation Image Knowing Who You Are In Christ.* Powerhouse Publishing, 1995.

Graham, Billy. *Answers to Life's Problems.* Grason, 1988.

Hegstrom, Paul. *Angry Men and the Women Who Love Them: Breaking the Cycle of Physical and Emotional Abuse.* Beacon Hill Press of Kansas City, 2004.

Hunt, June. *Domestic Violence: Assault on a Woman's Worth.* Aspire Press, 2013.

Hunt, June. *How to Rise above Abuse.* Harvest House Publishers, 2010.

Hunt, June. *Verbal & Emotional Abuse: Victory Over Verbal and Emotional Abuse.* Regent Publishing Services Ltd., 2017.

Jackson, John Paul. *Breaking Free of Rejection.* Streams Pub. House, 2004.

Jakes, T. D. Woman, *Thou Art Loosed! Healing the Wounds of the Past.* Destiny Image Publishers, 2012.

Jaynes, Sharon. *Enough: Silencing the Lies That Steal Your Confidence.* Harvest House Publishers, 2018.

King, Patricia. *Decree: Confessions from the Word of God to Strengthen Your Spirit.* Guardian Books, 2003.

Kroeger, Catherine Clark., and Nancy Nason-Clark. *No Place for Abuse: Biblical and Practical Resources to Counteract Domestic Violence.* IVP Books, 2010.

LaViolette, Alyce D., and Ola W. Barnett. *It Could Happen to Anyone: Why Battered Women Stay.* Sage Publications, 2000.

Leaf, Caroline. *Switch on Your Brain: the Key to Peak Happiness, Thinking, and Health.* Baker Books, 2013.

Leaf, Caroline. *Who Switched off Your Brain? Solving the Mystery of He Said/She Said.* Inprov, Ltd., 2011.

MacDonald, John. *Think Differently: Nothing Is Different Until You Think Differently - Bible Study Book.* Lifeway Christian Resources, 2016.

Miles, Al. *Domestic Violence: What Every Pastor Needs to Know.* Fortress Press, 2000.

Miller, John, and Glenna Miller. *Our Words of Faith Taking the Land.* Vision Publishing , 2005.

Mulholland, M. Robert. *Invitation to a Journey: a Road Map for Spiritual Formation.* InterVarsity, 1993.

Noll, Douglas E. *De-Escalate: How to Calm an Angry Person in 90 Seconds or Less.* Beyond Words Publishing, Incorporated, 2017.

Powlison, David. *Making All Things New: Restoring Joy to the Sexually Broken.* Crossway, 2017.

Rich, Phillip. T*he Power of Thanksgiving .* Ekklisia Ministries, 2011.

Sampson, Steve. *Breaking the Bondage Barrier: Taking the Limits of God. Sovereign World,* 1992.

Schaeffer, Brenda. *Is It Love or Is It Addiction?* Hazelden, 1987.

Sorge, Bob. *Dealing with the Rejection and Praise of Man.* Oasis House, 1999.

St. Cloud, Henry, and John Sims Townsend. *Boundaries: When to Say Yes, How to Say No to Take Control of Your Life.* Zondervan Books, 2012.

St. Cloud, Henry. *The Secret Things of God.* Howard Books, 2007.

St. Cloud, Henry, and Lisa Guest. *Changes That Heal: How to Understand Your Past to Ensure a Healthier Future.* Zondervan, 1994.

Standley, FIAMA, Loretta J. *And Who Are You?* Bloomington, IN, 2003.

Strong, James, et al. *The Strongest Strong's Exhaustive Concordance of the Bible.* Zondervan, 2001.

Tucker, Ronald D., and Rick Hufton. *Foundations for Christian Growth.* Grace Church: 1985.

United States, Congress, *Understanding the Nature and Dynamics of Domestic Violence*, 2007.

Van Rooyen, Leon. *Christian Character Balanced Living.* Forward Ministries, 2000.

Van Rooyen, Leon. *Christian Doctrine Rightly Dividing the Word of Truth.* Forward Ministries Bible Institute, 2000.

Van Rooyen, Leon. *Knowing God's Will and Voice Knowing and Doing God's Will.* Forward Ministries, 2000.

Waggoner, Brenda. *The Myth of the Submissive Christian Woman: Walking with God without Being Stepped on by Others.* Tyndale House Publishers, 2004.

Resources

1. Duluth Abuse of Children Wheel
www.theduluthmodel.org/wp-content/uploads/2017/03/Abuse- of-Children-2.pdf

2. Duluth Nurturing Children Wheel
www.theduluthmodel.org/wp-content/uploads/2017/03/ Nurturing-Children.pdf

3.Duluth Power and Control Wheel
www.theduluthmodel.org/wp-content/uploads/2017/03/ PowerandControl.pdf

4. Duluth Equality Wheel
www.theduluthmodel.org/wp-content/uploads/2017/03/ Equality.pdf

5. Safety Planning (page 201)

6. Safety Planning Websites:
www.thehotline.org/create-a-safety-plan/

7. Duluth Post Separation Wheel
www.theduluthmodel.org/wp-content/uploads/2017/03/Using-Children-Wheel.pdf

8. Controlling Relationship Assessment
www.guilford.com/add/forms/fontes3.pdf

9. Hurt by Love
www.hurtbylove.com/what-is-abuse-3/abuse-assessment/

10. L-O-V-E-S First Contact (page 195)

11. Additional Websites:
Domestic Shelters
www.domesticshelters.org

Faith Trust Institute
https://faithtrustinstitute.org

National Domestic Violence Hotline and 24-Hour Chatline
www.thehotline.org

National Domestic Violence Hotline Resources
www.thehotline.org/resources/

The National Coalition Against Domestic Violence
https://ncadv.org

National Domestic Violence Hotline: (800) 799- SAFE (7233)

First Contact

If You Suspect Abuse

You can start by letting her know you are worried someone is hurting her and are concerned for her safety. The following is a list of suggested questions.

- Do you feel loved, heard, and validated in your current relationship?

- Do you feel safe in your current relationship?

- Are you in a relationship where you are yelled at, called names, or accused of something you didn't do?

- Are you in a relationship with a person who threatens you or physically hurts you?

- Who caused these injuries? (if you see bruises, cuts, scratches, or other marks)

- Have you been kicked, hit, choked, or hurt by someone in the past year?

- Is your partner from a past relationship making you feel unsafe now?

If possible, have her fill out a relationship assessment. (See Resources 8 and 9)

When a Woman Discloses Abuse

- Pray for God to give you wisdom and safety. Pray for the right words to say to her. If you sense she is able to receive prayer at this time, ask God to give her the courage and strength she needs. Pray for her safety and the safety of her children. Pray for wisdom for her to make the best decision right now. If she is highly emotional or traumatized, she does not have to be included in the prayer at this point.

- Work with a team of support as soon as possible. This team may include law enforcement, domestic violence agencies, counselors, attorneys, and/or medical personnel. Avoid her dependence on or an emotional attachment to you or any other team member.

Victims want to have a voice that is heard. They want to have their feelings and experiences validated. They are reaching out for help and hope. It is critical each women is empowered and her decisions respected each step of the way. What seems the best decision to us may not be the best decision for her. Safety for her and her family is an ongoing concern.

==> **L**isten and believe her.
  - Let her tell her story her own way in her own time.
  - Avoid asking questions at this time.
  - Avoid reacting with strong emotions to what she tells you. You don't want her to assume guilt for your response.
  - Let her know how sorry you are that these things have happened to her. Let her know that what happened to her is not okay.
  - Do not minimize the danger she is in or what has happened.
  - Stay neutral as she talks about him; she may go back. She may remember your opinion of him and may assume your disapproval of her return making it harder for her reach out to you again.
  - Do not break confidentiality. You will lose her trust and may risk her safety. Do not tell *anyone* without her permission. Ask her permission to involve a mature, trusted Christian woman to help minister to her.

- Avoid spiritualizing the violence by focusing on religious issues at this time.
- Keep the focus on his responsibility for his actions.
- Listen for high risk words: weapons, previous and/or current threats to kill or commit suicide, sexual abuse, strangulation (often times incorrectly called choking), and stalking.

==> Offer **O**ptions.

- Ask about her immediate needs such as safety, child care, gas money, etc.
- Offer her information and options, not advice. Do not make decisions for her or insist she take certain actions she is not ready to make. Imposing your will can result in alienation, undue stress for the victim, and frustration if she decides to go back. (The average victim leaves 7 times.)
- Refer her as soon as possible to other agencies that can provide appropriate resources: shelter, police response, orders of protection, counseling, support groups, etc.
- Empower her to take action and make choices. Respect her decisions. She may not reach out immediately for additional help.
- Do not recommend couple's counseling, marriage enrichment seminars, mediation, communication workshops, or any other relationship counseling. This is not a relationship problem. It could further endanger the victim. (See Chapter 15)

==> **V**alidate her feelings.

- Acknowledge that her experiences should not have happened.
- Assure her that her feelings of fear, anger, sadness, depression, shame, guilt, worry, anxiety, frustration, sleepiness, dullness, detachment are all normal.
- Assure her that her that she is not crazy.

- Assure her that the abuse is not her fault nor does she deserve it
- Agree with her need for safety.
- State that his actions are wrong.
- Validate that his attitudes and actions need to change.
- Assert that abuse is never acceptable.

==> **E**ncourage her.
- Abuse is not God's will for her. A loving Father does not condone the abuse of His daughters.
- Assure her God is not punishing her.
- Assure her of the support of the church.
- Point out her strengths that will help her get through this.
- Leaving stops the cycle. Let her know that abuse occurs in cycles and often escalates in frequency and severity over time. Refer to the Cycle of Violence diagram in Chapter 9.
- Do assure her of God's love and presence.
- Assure her she did the right thing by coming to you. It takes great courage to expose an abuser.
- Thank her for trusting you enough to tell you what is happening.
- Help her establish trust by keeping your word, even in the smallest of things.

==> **S**afety plan.
- She has the right to be safe and to make decisions that are best for her and the children, not him.
- Address concerns about injuries. She may try to minimize them.
- Do not advise her to stay in or return to an unsafe environment. Place her safety above all other concerns. You can discuss the relationship later.
- Help her recognize the danger to herself and her children.

- Do not confront the abuser without her permission and a prayerfully considered plan.
- Do not go inside a home where active violence is occurring.
- If the situation is volatile, refer her to a shelter equipped with safety protocols. It is inadvisable to have her stay with a member of the congregation, possibly placing all at risk.
- Do not assume the marriage can be reconciled or she wants to reconcile. Domestic violence is a crime. Victims of crime are not sent back to the scene to become victims again.
- Respect her decisions whether she decides to stay or go. Change takes time. Let her know the church will be there for her on each step of her journey.
- Remember that leaving an abuser and being safe can be a long process. Separation does not mean safety as there is no guarantee the abuse won't continue. Leaving increases her risk of danger.
- Whether she decides to stay or leave, help her develop a safety plan that involves identifying action steps to increase her safety and to prepare in advance for the possibility of further violence. (See Resources 5 and 6)
- Request that she let someone know if he continues to threaten her safety or stalks her.

• If she decides to leave, help her mourn the loss to herself and her children.

• If she wants to reconcile, encourage her to wait for signs of change in him over an extended time period. Repentance and forgiveness are both the work of the Holy Spirit and must operate in God's timing, not man's. Go over the cycle of violence with her again as needed.

• Pray.

Listen

Options

Validate

Encourage

Safety

Safety Planning

Safety During an Argument

- Stay in an area with an exit and avoid letting the other person get between you and the exit.

- Practice getting out of your home safely.

- Avoid rooms with weapons, such as the kitchen.

- Have emergency 911 phones hidden throughout the home.

- Tell trustworthy neighbors about the violence. Ask them to call the police if they hear or see any disturbance.

- Devise a code word or signal to use with your children, family, friends, and trustworthy neighbors to indicate that you need the police.

- Do what you can to de-escalate the situation.

- Trust your instincts and judgment. You have the right to protect yourself until you are out of danger.

Safety When Preparing to Leave

- Work with people you trust to help make your plans.

- Establish your independence. Open savings and credit card accounts in your name only and specifically instruct institutions that your partner is not to have access. Have personal mail sent to a different address.

- Keep your purse and keys readily accessible at all times.

- Leave money, extra keys, copies of important documents, extra medicine and clothes with someone you trust so you can leave quickly.

- Review and rehearse your safety plan.

- Keep a packed bag at a trusted relative's or friend's home.

- Plan where you will go if you have to leave. Have a second location ready.

- Make arrangements for pets.

Safety in Your Own Home

- Change the locks on your doors. (Landlords in many states are legally obligated to change locks within 24 hours if you are experiencing domestic violence).

- Install or ask your landlord for increased security measures including locks and bars on your windows, replacing wooden doors with metal ones, additional locks for doors, installation of a security system, wedges for doors, etc.

- Devise escape routes from the second floor.

- Install smoke detectors and fire extinguishers on each level of the home.

- Discuss and practice a safety plan with your children for when you are not with them.

- Inform your children's schools or caregivers which people have permission to pick up your children.

- Inform trusted neighbors and your landlord that your partner no longer lives with you. Provide them with a picture of your partner and ask that they call the police if he is seen near your home.

- Teach your children how to call 911 or contact a safe person for help. Make sure they know the address.

- Position your vehicle in a way that allows for the quickest exit.
- Register with your state's Safe At Home program to protect your address.

Safety with a Protection Order

- Keep your Protection Order on you at all times.
- Inform trusted family, friends, neighbors, co-workers, and health care providers that you have a Protection Order in effect.
- Give a copy to a trusted neighbor, friend or family member, local law enforcement in areas you frequent.
- Give a copy to your children's schools or daycare.
- Call the police or file a police report if your abuser violates the Protection Order. Notify your attorney and others who have knowledge of your Order.
- Think of alternative ways to keep safe if the police do not respond right away.
- Document violations of the Protection Order. Include dates, times, what occurred, and any witnesses.

Safety on the Job and in Public

- Decide whom at work you will inform of your situation, include building security.
- Provide a photo of your abuser for quick identification.
- Screen your telephone calls.
- Devise a safety plan for leaving work, such as exiting through the back door.
- Have someone escort you when leaving and wait with you until you are safely en route.
- Use a variety of routes to go home from frequented places.

- Rehearse what you would do if something happened while going home, such as picking a safe place for yourself.
- Create a safety routine when you arrive home: checking your house and property, checking in with someone to let them know you are safe, etc.

Safety with Technology

- Use a phone to make or receive personal calls your partner cannot access, cannot access the billing records, or cannot change settings to track you.
- Use a computer your partner does not have access to seek help and resources.
- Arrange with government agencies, including the courts and mail service providers, to restrict access to your information.
- Change passwords on online accounts, including social media.
- Ask friends and family to refrain from giving out any information about you online.
- Find a trusted person familiar with technology to help you secure privacy and protection from any attempts by your partner to monitor your activities.

Safety and Your Emotional Health

- Identify whom you can rely on for emotional support. The National Domestic Violence Hotline number is (800) 799-SAFE (7233).
- Identify a trusted person you can call or spend time with before making decisions about returning to your partner.
- If you must communicate with your abuser, determine the safest way to do so and avoid being alone with him.

- Advocate for yourself and your needs. Find people and resources you can safely and openly talk to and ask for help. You are not alone, and you do not have to go through this by yourself.

- Look into counseling and support groups that directly address your experiences and needs.

- Find ways to care for yourself: exercise, make time to relax, create a safe environment, do things you enjoy, get as much support as you can.

Internet and Computer Safety

- Remember that all computer and online activity may be monitored.

- Abusers may monitor your emails and internet activity, if you are planning to flee to a particular location, don't look at classified ads for jobs and apartments, bus tickets, etc. for that place.

- It is safer to use a computer in a public library, at a trusted friend's house, at an internet cafe, or any other public terminals.

- Abusers may also track your activity and whereabouts through your cell phone; if you think there a chance this may be happening, take your phone into your provider, Apple store, or Best Buy Geek Squad and have it thoroughly checked.

- If your phone has been compromised and you get a new one, do NOT update your phone from the cloud.

Checklist: What You Should Take When You Leave

Legal Papers
- Restraining order/stalking order
- Lease, rental agreement, house deed
- Car registration

- Health and life insurance cards

- Divorce papers

- Custody papers

- Copies of police reports, photographs of injuries, and medical records

Identification

- Driver's license

- Passports

- Birth certificates

- Social security cards

- Self-sufficiency/disability identification

- Medical insurance cards

- Medicare/Medicaid cards

- Immigration information

Additional Papers

- Medical records for you and your children

- School and vaccination records

- Work permits/green card

- VISA

- Marriage, divorce, or separation papers

- Car registration and title

- Car loan/payment information

- Insurance papers

- Recent bank statements

- Recent credit card statements

- Latest tax return

- Lease, rental agreement, or house deed
- Mortgage payment information

Other

- House, work, and car keys
- Medications and medical supplies
- Cell phone and chargers
- Money, checkbook, bankbooks
- Debit, credit, and ATM cards
- Public assistance cards
- Valuables, photos, etc.
- Address book or written contact list
- Phone card/safety cell phone
- Clothes, security blankets, small toys for children
- Sentimental items
- Clothes, hygiene necessities, etc. for yourself
- Pictures of children
- Picture of partner
- Documentation of abuse including journals and photos

You are not alone!